THE COMMON SENSE APPROACH

Surviving

Puppyhood

D0963346

THE COMMON SENSE APPROACH

Surviving Puppyhood

Teaching Your Puppy the Right Way to Live

Kay Guetzloff

GULF PUBLISHING

Lanham • New York • Oxford

THE COMMON SENSE APPROACH

*S*urviving
*P*uppyhood

Copyright © 1999 by Gulf Publishing Company, Houston, Texas.
All rights reserved. This book, or parts thereof, may not be reproduced in
any form without express written permission of the publisher.

GULF PUBLISHING
An Imprint of the Rowman & Littlefield
Publishing Group
4501 Forbes Blvd., Suite 200
Lanham, MD 20706

Distributed by National Book Network
1-800-462-6420

Library of Congress Cataloging-in-Publication Data

Guetzloff, Kay.
    The common sense approach : surviving puppyhood :
teaching your puppy the right way to live / Kay Guetzloff.
        p.   cm.
    Includes index.
    ISBN 0-87719-353-3 (alk. paper)
    1. Puppies—Training.   2. Puppies—Behavior.   3. Puppies.
    I. Title.   II. Title: Surviving puppyhood
    SF431 .G85 1999
    636.7′0835—dc21   99-35848
                                                              CIP

Printed in the United States of America.
Printed on acid-free paper (∞).
Book design and illustrations by Roxann L. Combs.

Disclaimer

Dedication

I dedicate this book to all the dogs that have shared my life in the past and that share it in the present. They have taught me more than I have taught them. In particular, long gone but not forgotten are Siebe, my first obedience dog; Gretl, my first Obedience Champion; Rock, my first Border Collie; and most recently Sweep, once captain of the Heelalong soccer team and, as of this writing, the most winning obedience dog in the twentieth century.

Still living with us today are Kite, Wyn, and Lava, my obedience, herding, and agility partners.

I also want to thank my parents for raising me with discipline and love and for teaching me the right way to live. I have tried to follow their teachings throughout my life.

Finally, my heartfelt thanks to my husband, Dick, for his patience and understanding. There have been many times when I was writing this book or when I was involved in other dog activities that I had no time to go to the grocery store or wash clothes. I could always count on Dick to help out, and I am extremely grateful for his support.

Discipline Is Love

For the good of your dog
you must understand
That discipline and love
go hand in hand.

It's easier by far
to pamper your pet
Than to constantly strive
to teach him respect.

But puppies, like babies,
all have to grow up
And deal with the world
as dogs, not as pups.

So greater than love
is the gift you can give
By teaching your dog
The right way to live.

This poem was written by Linda Decker of Illinois, on
January 28, 1984, and presented to Kay Guetzloff with
the following tribute: "For Kay, a teacher, a friend, and a
no-nonsense lady, with thanks for the know-how you're
constantly sharing."

Contents

Acknowledgments

I would like to thank my many dog training students, present and past, who gave me ideas for this book and who also suggested the book's title. In particular, I wish to thank Jann Cooper and Margaret Dunfee for the many hours they spent reading for content and editing my "English" for the American market. In addition, my thanks to the Reverend Joleen DuBois and her Sheltie, Anasazi, of White Mountain for their participation in the training pictures, along with photographer Shary Singer. Also thanks to photographer Nelson Enochs for taking the remainder of the training pictures and to all those who sent me pictures to use for each chapter. Finally, my thanks to Margret Taylor for providing me with the two wonderful pictures of her dog, Molly, for the front cover of this book.

Introduction

Since the dawn of time, humans have shared their homes with dogs. In the beginning, people kept dogs as hunters or guardians. Humans quickly discovered that some dogs were better at hunting than others, and so those dogs were bred and produced even better hunting dogs. Similarly, the dogs humans owned that were better at protecting the settlement were bred together, and even better guardians were produced. Then, humans took this one step further. Some dogs were better at hunting birds and others at tracking game. Like was bred to like, and breeds were developed for different uses, like duck dogs, pheasant dogs, rabbit dogs, and coon dogs.

Today, humans have no need of a dog to bring food to the table, although some dogs are still used for hunting as a sport. Through natural selection, dogs are used as guardians of flocks or to move flocks and herds from one area to another. Police and customs agents use dogs to sniff for drugs. Search and rescue groups use dogs to help locate disaster victims. Dogs have been bred to lead the blind and are used to alert deaf persons to the ring of the telephone or doorbell. However, dog's greatest achievement is that of companion, a function that he has performed well for centuries.

There is nothing more rewarding than raising a dog from puppyhood to old age. The benefits that dog ownership brings far outnumber the problems often associated with owning a dog. Dogs give their owners unconditional love. No matter how poorly they are treated, dogs always appear to love their owners. Older citizens who own dogs often live longer than non-dog owners of the same age. There is scientific proof that when a person strokes a dog or a cat the person's blood pressure is lowered. A burglar is less likely to break into a house if there is a dog in residence. Latchkey children enjoy the companionship a dog brings when they go home to an empty house after school. The list goes on and on.

Sadly, not all puppies survive puppyhood. Some puppies succumb to poor genetics or classic canine diseases. However, with proper breeding and inoculations these problems should be minimal. Some puppies fall victim to accidents. Taking the proper precautions to raise the puppy in a safe environment can prevent this. Unfortunately, some perfectly healthy puppies end up as a statistic at the pound simply because the owners got tired of them.

Both people and dogs can survive puppyhood, with a little planning on the part of the human. First, a potential dog owner should try to select a puppy to suit his lifestyle. If you choose a high-energy breed, and you spend your life on the couch in front of the TV, it is obvious that there will be trouble ahead. With lack of exercise your puppy may become frustrated and destroy your home. Should he do that, he may not survive. Once a puppy takes up residence in your home, it is your responsibility to teach him the right way to live. Unsupervised, a puppy will do all things canine. This could include digging holes, chewing on wood and walls, chasing livestock or vehicles, and biting the mail carrier. Should this happen, your dog is not being a bad puppy, but he does need to be better trained. To tell the truth, you have not done your part in the education process, and it is up to you to do something to turn things around.

The focus of this book is to assist the reader in selecting a dog that will fit in with his lifestyle and then, through the use of discipline, love, and training, to help both the owner and dog to survive puppyhood by teaching the puppy the right way to live.

Author's Note

In this book, we named our generic puppy "Einstein." Many dog owners are convinced they own the smartest dog in the world, and so that is why we chose this name.

If you have not already chosen a name for your puppy, I would recommend you select the name with care. When people give their dogs particular names, they sometimes get what they choose. A number of years ago, I had a client whose family owned a small, fluffy breed known for its sweet and affectionate nature. As a joke, the family members named their dog "Killer." My introduction to Killer was on the first night of puppy class when she promptly tried to remove several fingers from my hand. Killer and I quickly came to an understanding, but I was the only person aside from members of her family to be able to touch her. Killer had to be sedated before any visit to the veterinarian, and for the twelve years of her life, her owners had to plan her grooming appointments and their vacations around my schedule. Killer is only one of a number of dogs that I can think of whose owners named them inappropriately. Many of these dogs went on to become what their names implied.

All the anecdotes in this book are true. Only the names of the dogs (and their breeds) have been changed to protect the innocent (owner).

CHAPTER 1

The Cost of Puppy Love

If you are in the market for a pet, the first question you should ask yourself is "Why do I want to own a dog?" Depending on your answer, you may decide you would be better off with some other type of pet or no pet at all.

If you ask dog owners why they have dogs, they are likely to answer, "For companionship and security." Even the barking of a dog as small as a Yorkshire Terrier can be a deterrent to someone about to enter your home without your permission. A barking dog can alert you to the fact that something is going on outside so you can take appropriate action. If you enjoy running and hiking, taking a dog along when you go out minimizes the chance of being attacked. A walk is much more enjoyable when shared with a dog.

◀ Even a brush, bath, and blow-dry comes at a price and needs to be figured into your doggie budget. Best in Show Pekingese, Ch. Claymore Opening Night, bred and owned by Mrs. Robert I. Ballenger. *Photo by Luke Allen. Pekingese, Toy Group.*

1

Perhaps your favorite pastime is hunting; you may wish to buy one of the sporting breeds to share your hobby. These are some of the many reasons people choose to live with Man's Best Friend.

If you are considering getting a dog because of pleas from a child, do think this over carefully. As long as you want to own a dog too, choose a breed that will make a good companion for children. A dog often becomes a child's best friend, especially a child who does not have any brothers and sisters. However, do not expect your child to take full responsibility for the care and feeding of the dog. You will need to oversee it. Also, consider how quickly children tire of their Christmas toys. There is no canine Toys for Tots program where you can recycle the dog at a later date if your child becomes tired of him. Be sure to choose a breed that you will enjoy should your child lose interest or move away from home.

Some people fall in love with a "dog-star" on television or at the movies and then go out and buy a dog just like it. They forget that the dog that plays a role is really a fantasy, and an extremely well-trained one at that. It is not a "real" dog, any more than the show portrays real life. I once received a call from one of my clients who was upset with her dog. She owned a large mixed-breed of average intelligence that had successfully completed one of my obedience classes. She also had a small child. One day the dog and the child were playing in the fenced backyard when the little girl managed to unlatch the gate and go out in front of the house, while the dog remained in the back. A neighbor found the child standing in the street and took her to her mother. My client called me because she wanted to know how she could train Bonzo to alert her when her child was in danger. I told her I did not think it would be possible to train any dog to do that. Her response was, "If Bonzo had been smart like Lassie, he would have come and found me." We do not realize what impact television has on our lives and how we tend to believe what we see, although we should know much of it is fantasy.

Now that you have made a decision to own a dog, you should consider some of the costs involved in dog ownership. Dogs are similar to automobiles in that it is not the initial cost of the dog that should be of concern, but the cost of maintenance. Many puppies acquired through shelters may cost very little to adopt. A purebred puppy bought at a pet shop most likely will be of poor quality. However, a pet shop puppy is likely to be more expensive than a quality purebred dog acquired directly from a reputable breeder. If the average life span of a dog is ten years, and the cost to buy a particular dog is $500, then you are looking at spending $50 a year for the pleasure of owning a particular dog. A well-bred dog may cost more to buy than a poorly bred dog, but if you average the cost over ten years, the difference is not going to be significant. With dogs as with most anything else, you usually get what you pay for. However, if your car is a lemon you can trade it in for a different model. You cannot trade in a dog.

The initial purchase price of the dog is one of your least considerations. Feeding, grooming, and veterinary expenses, among other things, may cost a lot more than you bargained for unless you take care in selecting the right dog. Some dogs look at a sack of dog food and gain five pounds. Others eat you out of house and home, sometimes quite literally, and still look as though they spent a year on a starvation diet. Feeding quality dog food can be expensive, but if you try to feed your dog something cheaper he could end up with bowel, skin, or coat problems, which will necessitate a trip to the vet. Some dogs live their entire lives visiting the vet for only routine inoculations. However, some people get to know their vets on a first-name basis because they have to take their dogs to see them so often. Some breeds are much healthier than others, so the selection of a healthy breed will save you money in the long run.

Some breeds require professional grooming. Many dog owners take their dogs to the doggie equivalent of Vidal Sassoon. In this busy day and age, few of us set aside enough time to brush and bathe our own dogs. Even a brush, bath, and blow-dry at Canine Supercuts comes at a price and needs to be figured into your doggie budget. A dog groomer bases her fee on the time it takes her to do the job. It takes several hours to groom a Standard Poodle, unless you want him given a buzz-job. Grooming charges for a regular cut are likely to be in excess of $75, every six to eight weeks. The cost to groom an Old English Sheepdog is likely to be higher still. Puppy coats of all breeds are considerably easier to groom than the adult coat, and you may be able to cope in the beginning. However, you may be in for a rude awakening when you take your dog to the canine beauty salon for the first time if you have chosen a breed that requires the services of a professional groomer. For financial reasons, you may want to consider choosing a breed that requires minimum coat care so that you can bathe him yourself.

It would be wonderful if dogs came out of the womb as well-trained as Lassie. Since they do not, you are the one who will have to turn a canine Einstein into the type of companion you desire. Many dog owners enjoy attending obedience class with their pets. Do not forget to figure the cost of dog training class, and possibly some special training equipment, into your budget.

Another cost associated with dog ownership is the problem of what to do with your dog if you need to go out of town. Relying on your neighbor to look after your puppy may not be a good move. A dog left home alone for an extended period is likely to get bored. No matter how well-trained your dog might be, he could start chewing on your belongings or begin barking and howling out of sheer frustration at being left behind. Therefore, you may need to figure boarding expenses into your vacation budget.

Most dog owners consider tumbleweed fur-balls drifting around their houses a small price to pay for the love of a dog. Remember that if a dog joins your household you may need to allow additional time to clean up after muddy paw prints. You can always remove doggie nose prints from your glass doors and windows with Windex.

The next important question to ask is yourself is "What type of dog would suit my lifestyle?"

CHAPTER 2

A Dog for All Reasons

Selecting the right dog to suit your lifestyle is a recipe for success. Going out and getting just any dog can be a recipe for disaster. Shelters and humane societies are filled to capacity with dogs that someone did not select with enough care. This should not happen to you if you select a dog to suit your lifestyle and then take the time to teach him house manners and social graces.

Over the centuries dogs have been genetically programmed to behave in a certain way. Some dogs were bred to live in cold climates while others were bred to live in the desert. Some breeds are small enough to fit in a woman's purse while others are large enough for a two-year-old to ride. An Irish Wolfhound is not a suitable breed for apartment living, nor is a Yorkshire Terrier suitable

◀ Somewhere out there is a breed to suit your lifestyle. You just need to find the right one. Hollyhill's Frn'dly Persuasion CD, owned by Ruth Hertzog. *Photo by Laura Berger. Labrador Retriever, Sporting Group.*

for life on a cattle ranch. Somewhere out there is a breed to suit your lifestyle. You just need to find the right one.

There are ten questions you need to ask yourself, and the answers may steer you in the direction of a suitable breed. Take time to answer these questions before you start your quest to find the perfect puppy. There may be several breeds that appeal to you, so further investigation may be needed to narrow down your choice.

A question of major importance is **"Are there children in the family, and if so, what are their ages?"** Remember that you are buying the dog for yourself, but you must also select a breed that will be trustworthy around children.

If your children are under the age of ten, a puppy from the Toy Group would not be a good choice. (See Table 3-2, p. 19.) Toy dogs are very fragile and easily injured. Children love to carry puppies around, and it is easy to pick up a toy dog. However, they are just as easy to drop. A better choice for a family with children would be a more robust breed, like a Labrador. I once had a client who offered to look after her neighbor's Toy Poodle puppy. My client had two little boys who slept in bunk beds. The children were used to taking their toys up to the upper bunk, and the puppy was small, light, and easy to lift. The boys never thought about the puppy wanting to get down from the upper bunk—their toys always stayed put. Unfortunately, when the puppy jumped off the top bunk he broke both front legs. Had the puppy been a more robust breed he would have been too heavy to lift, and this accident would never have happened.

Another important question is **"Do you live in an urban, suburban, or rural setting?"** If you live in the city, a dog's exercise requirements are of major importance. A dog with a high energy level is not a good apartment dweller. You need to select a breed that prefers to lie by the fire rather than chase the squirrels in the park. However, if you live in the country, a German Shorthaired Pointer might be a perfect choice of dog.

"**Do you spend every weekend hiking the Appalachian Trail?**" If you were looking for a canine hiking partner, a Bulldog would hardly be the right choice. You should consider one of the more athletic breeds, like a Doberman Pinscher or a Border Collie.

"**Are you a disciplinarian?**" If you want a dog that will salute and stand to attention every time you issue an order, do not consider a terrier. Disobedience is often the terrier's forte, and in addition, they have a great sense of humor. Terriers make great pets for people who do not take life too seriously.

"**Do you travel a lot on business or vacation?**" If you know you will have to leave your dog at the Holidog Inn on occasion, make sure you select a breed that is not owner dependent. Some breeds, such as the German Shepherd Dog, are difficult to board. These dogs are so attached to their owners that they often go into decline when left at a kennel. They are convinced their owners have abandoned them and will not even eat, consequently becoming sick from the stress of separation. Some dog owners decide to use the services of a house sitter instead of a kennel. However, some breeds will not allow a house sitter to come into the house to take care of them once the owner has left. What are you going to do if this situation arises when you are halfway around the world?

"**Do you spend long hours at work?**" If you do, you really should consider owning a pet that does not require much attention. However, if you simply must have a canine companion, select a breed that will be happy lying on the couch all day long. Some of the toy breeds or perhaps an English Bulldog would fit the bill.

"**Are you retired, and do you therefore spend much of the year traveling?**" RV parks and motels have fewer restrictions on small breeds than they do large ones. In addition, small dogs take up a lot less space in a motor home or fifth wheel. As you get older your physical strength diminishes, and a smaller breed will be easier for you to handle.

"In which geographical part of the country do you live?"
Dogs with short coats are better suited to living in the southern part
of the United States. A Whippet would not survive well in the
Minnesota winters. However, a Siberian Husky would be happier
living in Minnesota than Arizona. If your dog is going to spend time
outdoors, choose a breed that has the right coat for the climate in
which he will be living. Some breeds adapt to any climate, while
others are miserable if the weather is too hot, too cold, or too wet.

"How big are you?" If you only weigh one hundred pounds
soaking wet, think twice about getting a dog that weighs more
than you do. Even a dog as small as sixty pounds can sometimes be
difficult for a woman to handle. You should choose a breed that
you can physically control.

**"Who else in your family group will have to deal with your
dog?"** Perhaps your heart is set on owning a Maltese Terrier, but
your significant other is the one who will be in charge of the
puppy's daily exercise. Your partner, who looks like a linebacker for
the Chicago Bears, may feel uncomfortable walking such an effem-
inate dog. A rugged Cairn Terrier might be a better choice if you
want to own a small breed of dog.

You may need to ask yourself some additional questions since
you know your lifestyle better than anyone. A little forethought
may mean the difference between failure and success in your dealings with Man's Best Friend.

PUREBRED VS. RANDOM-BRED

You may wonder if you should buy a purebred dog. You have
probably heard that mixed-breed dogs are healthier than purebreds. The fact is that some purebred dogs will be healthier than
some mixed-breeds, and some mixed-breeds will be healthier than
some purebreds. A lot depends on the genetic mix of the dog. Any

veterinarian will tell you that the same health issues occur in pure-bred and random-bred dogs. Mixed-breed dogs do develop hip dysplasia, thyroid problems, cancer, and blindness, as do their pure-bred counterparts.

The advantage of owning a purebred dog over a mixed-breed is that dogs of the same breed tend to behave in like manner. For centuries, dogs have been selected for certain traits. Any type of retriever worth his rawhide will bring back anything you throw for him, except food! A cross between a retriever and a Beagle might look more like a retriever. However, when you throw a ball for your dog to fetch, he might return with a rabbit instead. If a retriever is your choice, you should expect him to have a retriever personality. You never know what sort of personality you will get if you adopt a random-bred dog. A random-bred dog will cost as much to raise and train as a purebred, but he might have a personality that you find hard to live with.

MALE VS. FEMALE

Whether you choose a male or female dog is often a matter of personal preference. Many people find that a female dog is easier to live with. Female dogs, known as bitches, are less likely to urinate in your house than males, and they are often more compliant when it comes to training. The trainability of your dog is often based on the breed you have chosen. In addition, bitches tend to be smaller than males and therefore easier to handle, if size is a factor in your choice of dog. If you have decided that you will only consider a puppy of a certain sex, be sure to check the puppy's gender for yourself before you take him (or her) home. You would be surprised how many people are unaware of how to tell the difference between a male and female puppy. Several years ago the following story was related to me by one of my students. It is both funny and hard to believe.

My student Dodie was out in the yard one day and noticed that her neighbor had acquired a puppy. In the course of their conversation, Dodie asked her neighbor what she had decided to call the puppy, and she learned the name was Maggie. Several days later my friend was working in her garden, pulling up weeds along the fence. Maggie came out in the yard and, in typical puppy fashion, came fawning over to my friend for a scratch on the belly. When Maggie rolled over onto her back, my friend noticed that Maggie had a penis. The neighbor came over to chat, and Dodie said, "Didn't you tell me you named your puppy Maggie?" When the neighbor concurred, my friend said, "Maggie is a name for a girl dog, and you have a boy dog." The neighbor looked startled and asked Dodie for an explanation. My friend told her, "Male dogs have 'handles'; your puppy has a handle" and indicated the penis. Then Dodie gave the neighbor a lesson in canine anatomy, using two of her dogs as models. The neighbor had never owned a dog, not even while growing up, and believed the only way to tell the difference between a male and female puppy was because a male lifted his leg to urinate. So when she looked at a litter of puppies and saw Maggie squat to urinate, she selected her. Male dogs do lift their legs, but not when they're as young as seven weeks of age. Needless to say, Maggie was renamed.

NEUTERING

If you neuter your dog, many unpleasant male habits can be eliminated. Male dogs neutered early in life will often squat to urinate rather than lift their legs on bushes, trees, and the occasional bedspread. Without male hormones circulating around his body, a neutered male will be less likely to get into fights or to go in search of female companionship. In addition, a neutered male will have less chance of succumbing to two serious canine health issues—

cancer of the prostate in addition to cancer of the testes. Today, neutering is a simple and inexpensive operation. However, if your puppy has a retained testicle then the operation becomes more complex.

Many owners underestimate their dogs' desire for procreation, and this desire can often lead to heartache. A number of years ago I had a student with an intact male dog that showed great promise as an obedience competitor. "Romeo" was a flirt, and his owner was talking about getting him neutered. Before she had a chance to do so, Romeo somehow got out of the fenced yard and went in search of romance. The moment my student noticed her dog was missing, she took off in search of him. Unfortunately, she found him too late. He had been hit by a car while crossing the street some distance from her house. Most pet dogs are not streetwise, and Romeo was no exception. Had my student neutered Romeo early in life he probably would have had no desire for female companionship. A dog's sense of smell is all-powerful. Intact male dogs can become frustrated when they smell a bitch in heat. They will howl, pant, ignore their food, and often lift their legs in the house. In a wild pack, only the alpha (top) dog may breed. Your puppy, Einstein, will be a much happier pet when not subjected to sexual urges. The only way to prevent this is by having him neutered, and as early as possible.

SPAYING

An unspayed bitch usually comes "in heat" twice a year. This heat period lasts approximately twenty-one days. During this time you can never allow her access to the outdoors without riding shotgun over her since a determined canine caller will find a way over, through, around, or under any barrier placed in his way. When in your house, a female in heat will have to wear the doggie equivalent of Kotex. Otherwise, you will need to confine her to her crate unless you want to have your carpets cleaned at the end of her cycle. Spaying your bitch is a simple and inexpensive operation that comes with added health benefits. A bitch spayed before her first heat cycle is not inclined to get breast cancer. A female dog without reproductive organs is likely to be healthier than one that can produce.

INSIDE OR OUTSIDE DOG?

You have already learned that dog's greatest achievement is that of being a companion to man. An outside dog costs just as much to keep as an inside dog. Why would you want the expense of owning a dog if all you do is see him once in a while when you step out into the yard? How can your dog fulfill his role of companion if he never spends time with you? Some people get a dog for protection. How can your dog offer you protection when locked away from you on the other side of the door?

Some people keep their dogs outside because the dog is destroying items in the house. However, even in the yard your dog will find plenty of objects to destroy. Garden hoses, clothes hung on the washing line, shrubbery, and siding are all tempting chew toys. We once had a client whose dog chewed the landau top of his Cadillac when the car was parked in the driveway. I never did hear if his auto insurance covered the destruction. I wonder if a claim would be made under vandalism, canine not human.

If you want a dog to live outdoors then you need to select the breed very carefully. Toy breeds are not suited to living outdoors. They need and expect pampering. Some dogs left outside become nuisance barkers, which will cause you problems with your neighbors. I once had a student who kept his four-month-old puppy outside during the day when he was at work. One night in class he brought up the subject of barking and asked what to do about it.

The obvious answer was to keep the puppy indoors, but his spouse would not agree. A week later I got a call from the same student to tell me he had to drop out of the class. It was not that he found my answer to his problem unsatisfactory; a neighbor had tired of the barking and had thrown poison over the fence. My student's dog had just became one of those puppies that did not survive puppyhood.

Now that you have given some thought as to what type of lifestyle you lead, it is time to look at the different types of dogs available to share your home.

CHAPTER 3

From Chihuahuas to Great Danes

Before you go in search of a puppy, take time to list the things you require in a dog and the things you would prefer not to have. Put these two columns side by side so that you can contrast your likes and dislikes. (See Table 3-1.)

When you read about the different dog breeds, you can determine if they fit your criteria by checking your list. However, be prepared to modify your needs. Remember that there is no perfect dog, just a breed that will suit your lifestyle better than some other breed you may be considering.

◀ In 1999, the American Kennel Club recognized 148 different breeds or varieties of purebred dogs. The Chihuahua is the smallest breed, and the Great Dane is one of the largest. Top Photo: *Photo by Mary Sue Gill. Chihuahua, Toy Group*. Bottom Photo: Ch. Simmons Garrett CDX, CGC, owned by Nancy Simmons. *Photo by Nancy Simmons. Great Dane, Working Group.*

TABLE 3-1
A SAMPLE CHART SHOWING LIKES AND DISLIKES

Must have/be	Do not want
Under 40 lbs.	A dog that requires professional grooming
Low energy level	The expense of putting up a fence
Good with children	A dog that barks excessively

If you are considering acquiring a purebred dog, the choice of breeds available is enormous. In 1999 the American Kennel Club, which is the largest registry of purebred dogs in the United States, recognized 148 different breeds or varieties of purebred dogs. From time to time, the AKC will add more breeds to this number. The United Kennel Club, which is the second largest registry body in the United States, recognizes many of the same and some additional breeds not recognized by AKC. Furthermore, there are breeds not yet recognized by either of these organizations that may suit your requirements. Eventually either the AKC, the UKC, or both organizations will accept some of these "rare" breeds for registration. Notice the use of the words *registry* and *registration*. Unknowledgeable dog owners equate registration with quality. This is far from the case. The main purpose of AKC and UKC is to register dogs. In addition, these organizations hold dog shows. Just because your dog is registered does not necessarily mean your dog has the potential to be a "show" dog. The registration papers you receive when you buy a purebred puppy only tell you that the parents of the puppy you bought are registered and that your puppy is entitled to registration. It does not mean the puppy you bought is necessarily a good specimen of his breed.

Since you have to start somewhere in your quest for a dog, take a look at the breeds to be found in the seven American Kennel Club groups (See Table 3-2.). To begin with, you might go to the local library and read the AKC's *Complete Dog Book*, which gives a brief description of the different breeds the AKC accepts for registration. You can also visit their Web site on the Internet (www.akc.org). There you can find information on the parent club of many of the different breeds. If you then visit the breed club, you can get more specific information than is found in many books. Breed sites often include breeder referral and rescue information. Each year in March, AKC ranks the most popular to the least popular breeds of dogs registered with the organization during the previous calendar year. For good reason, many of the breeds listed in the top ten have remained popular for some time. Other breeds only remain in the top ten for a year or two and then return to obscurity. Breeds that suddenly become fashionable and then just as quickly lose their popularity are called "fad" or "yuppie" breeds. There is a good explanation for their quick demise. For one reason or another, fad breeds seldom make good pets for the average dog owner.

TABLE 3-2
BREEDS AND GROUPS RECOGNIZED BY THE AMERICAN KENNEL CLUB, WITH THE BREEDS LISTED IN ALPHABETICAL ORDER WITHIN THE GROUPS

Sporting Group

American Water Spaniel
Brittany
Chesapeake Bay Retriever
Clumber Spaniel
Cocker Spaniel (3 color varieties)
Curly Coated Retriever
English Cocker Spaniel
English Springer Spaniel
English Setter
Field Spaniel
Flat Coated Retriever
German Shorthaired Pointer
German Wirehaired Pointer
Golden Retriever
Gordon Setter
Irish Setter
Irish Water Spaniel
Labrador Retriever
Pointer
Sussex Spaniel
Vizsla
Weimaraner
Welsh Springer Spaniel
Wirehaired Pointing Griffon

Hound Group

Afghan Hound
Basenji
Basset Hound
Beagle (2 varieties by height)
Black and Tan Coonhound
Bloodhound
Borzoi
Dachshund (3 coat varieties)
Foxhound, American
Foxhound, English
Greyhound

Harrier
Ibizan Hound
Irish Wolfhound
Norwegian Elkhound
Otterhound
Petit Basset Griffon Vendeen
Pharaoh Hound
Rhodesian Ridgeback
Saluki
Scottish Deerhound
Whippet

Working Group

Akita
Alaskan Malamute
Bernese Mountain Dog
Boxer
Bullmastiff
Doberman Pinscher
Giant Schnauzer
Great Dane
Great Pyrenees
Greater Swiss Mountain Dog

Komondor
Kuvasz
Mastiff
Newfoundland
Portuguese Water Dog
Rottweiler
Saint Bernard
Samoyed
Siberian Husky
Standard Schnauzer

Terrier Group

Airedale Terrier
American Staffordshire Terrier
Australian Terrier
Bedlington Terrier
Border Terrier
Bull Terrier (2 varieties)
Cairn Terrier
Dandie Dinmont Terrier
Fox Terrier (Smooth)
Fox Terrier (Wire)
Irish Terrier
Kerry Blue Terrier
Lakeland Terrier

Manchester Terrier
Miniature Bull Terrier
Miniature Schnauzer
Norfolk Terrier
Norwich Terrier
Scottish Terrier
Sealyham Terrier
Skye Terrier
Soft Coated Wheaten Terrier
Staffordshire Bull Terrier
Welsh Terrier
West Highland White Terrier

Toy Group

Affenpinscher	Manchester Terrier (Toy)
Brussels Griffon	Miniature Pinscher
Cavalier King Charles Spaniel	Pomeranian
Chihuahua (2 coat varieties)	Papillon
Chinese Crested	Pekingese
English Toy Spaniel	Poodle (Toy)
Havanese	Pug
Italian Greyhound	Shih Tzu
Japanese Chin	Silky Terrier
Maltese	Yorkshire Terrier

Non-sporting Group

American Eskimo Dog	Keeshond
Bichon Frise	Lhasa Apso
Boston Terrier	Lowchen
Bulldog	Poodle (2 varieties)
Chinese Shar-pei	Schipperke
Chow Chow	Shiba Inu
Dalmatian	Tibetan Spaniel
Finnish Spitz	Tibetan Terrier
French Bulldog	

Herding Group

Australian Cattle Dog	Canaan Dog
Australian Shepherd	Collie (2 varieties, Smooth and Rough)
Bearded Collie	
Belgian Malinois	German Shepherd Dog
Belgian Sheepdog	Old English Sheepdog
Belgian Tervuren	Puli
Border Collie	Shetland Sheepdog
Bouvier Des Flandres	Welsh Corgi (Cardigan)
Briard	Welsh Corgi (Pembroke)

Miscellaneous Group (breeds awaiting AKC recognition)

Anatolian Shepherd	Jack Russell Terrier
Italian Spinoni	Plott Hound

Source: *Rules Applying to Dog Shows,* Chapter 3, "Dog Show Classifications," American Kennel Club.

In addition to the breed popularity charts, each April the AKC lists the number of breed championships and titles earned in performance events during the previous calendar year. Even if competing in performance events is the farthest thing from your mind, these statistics should be of great interest to you in your search for the perfect puppy. First, take a look at the obedience statistics. Some breeds earn very few obedience titles, while others earn many advanced titles. Obedience titles indicate that a breed is trainable to a certain degree. Take a look at the hunting breeds. Some sporting or hound breeds earn many hunting titles, while others earn hardly any. By studying these statistics, you will discover whether the breed that interests you retains many of his genetic instincts or whether that breed is a hound or sporting breed in name only. Breeds that earn many agility titles show they have both trainability and stamina. Breeds credited with many titles in agility might need more exercise than breeds that earn few agility titles. Obviously, a popular breed is likely to have earned more titles than other breeds in the same group. Therefore, when you look at the number of titles listed, take into account the popularity of the breed. Some of the not-so-popular breeds often earn a higher percentage of titles than their more popular cousins. Accordingly, you might want to consider one of these less popular breeds if trainability or genetic makeup is a major concern to you.

When a breed stays popular for a number of years, it is often over-bred and likely to have health problems. People often decide to cash in on a breed's popularity and do not breed for quality, but quantity instead. Through lack of knowledge, they breed dogs with genetic problems like hip dysplasia, thyroid problems, and seizures to name a few. The careful selection of any breeder will minimize potential health problems in your puppy.

It is impossible to go into details about all the 148 breeds of dogs recognized at this time by AKC. Therefore, let us concentrate on the more popular members of the various groups. If you become interested in a breed low in the popularity charts, be aware that you may have to wait for months or even a year or more to get a puppy of that breed. Most people, once they decide to get a dog, are not willing to wait long for the right puppy to come along. By selecting a more popular breed, your chances are better of finding the right puppy fairly quickly.

THE SPORTING GROUP

Pointers, retrievers, setters, and spaniels make up the Sporting Group. Sporting dogs enjoy an overall more masculine appeal than some other groups. Their coats range from no-maintenance (the Vizsla) to hard to groom (the American Cocker Spaniel). There is enough of a size range in the Sporting Group to satisfy both the urban and rural dwellers. Dogs in the Sporting Group have been bred to hunt alongside man and to go out in the field with other dogs. For this reason, most sporting dogs are not dog-aggressive, and they generally get along well with people.

The three most popular breeds in the Sporting Group are the American Cocker Spaniel, the Labrador Retriever, and the Golden Retriever. Both the Labrador and Golden Retrievers make good family dogs. They are usually trustworthy around children. The Lab is probably more popular because of his short coat, but in fact he sheds much more than the Golden. Labs are heavy year-round shedders, whereas the Golden is seasonal. The Golden Retriever is likely to be more energetic than some Labradors. However, many Labs and Goldens today are better acquainted with a hearthrug than a duck pond. There are two types of Labradors and Goldens— field and show/pet. The field dogs will be much more active than the other type, so be sure you know what type you are getting if you decide a retriever is the breed for you. You do not want to get a retriever from field lines if you are looking for a dog to live in an urban setting, one that will spend the evening sleeping in front of the fire. As testament to their good nature and trainability, both the Labrador and Golden retrievers are popular breeds chosen to lead the blind.

The American Cocker Spaniel is one of the most appealing puppies on which you will ever lay your eyes. Unfortunately, the American Cocker has numerous health problems. If you decide to own one you will probably contribute to the rent on your local veterinary hospital each month. Many Cockers suffer from ear, eye, and skin problems, and they do not always have the best temperaments. In addition, their coats need professional grooming. You might wonder why they remain such popular dogs. There is probably no good answer for that, except they are an ideal size for urban dwellers. They do not need a great deal of exercise to keep them happy.

If the retriever breeds appeal to you, one of the best kept secrets in the Sporting group is the Flat Coated Retriever. If you are looking for an occasional hunting companion, a Flat Coat will do an adequate job for you. They are as good with the family as the Lab and the Golden, and with less coat than a Golden, they are easy to groom. They are versatile enough to train for performance events, and do well at all of them. If there is a disadvantage to owning a Flat Coat it is that the breed suffers from cancer, and many die much earlier than one would wish.

Many of the less popular pointers and setters continue to be used for hunting, in addition to a role of family companion. They have a higher energy level than many of the retrievers and require more exercise. For that reason, they are not the breed for an urban setting. Setters from hunting stock have shorter coats than those from show lines and seldom require the services of a professional groomer. The Irish Setter is one of the most attractive-looking dogs in the Sporting Group. However, because of its beauty, people have bred the Irish to be more of a show dog than a hunting dog. Irish Setters are clowns that do not take life or training very seriously, and most Irish setters require occasional professional grooming.

The German Shorthaired and German Wirehaired pointers are versatile hunters used either for retrieving ducks from icy ponds or pointing upland birds. Overall, German breeds tend to be a little stubborn, but these pointers do make good family dogs and are easier to train than many of the setters. Furthermore, their coats are low maintenance. As with many of the other sporting dogs, they do need a considerable amount of exercise. Another excellent choice is the Vizsla. This breed is increasing in popularity, being similar to the German Shorthair in size, coat, and exercise requirements. The Vizsla is one of the more trainable breeds in the Sporting Group and is a pretty gold color with amber eyes. Another pointing breed is the Weimaraner, often called "the gray ghost" because of its unusual gray color. This breed is more dominant than the aforementioned pointers and needs a firm hand. It would not necessarily be the best choice for a first-time dog owner.

The Brittany looks more like a spaniel, but it is classed as a pointer. This is a medium-sized dog with a pretty, silky medium-length coat. Brittanys are easier to train than many of the sporting breeds. Because of their smaller size, you might expect they would make a good urban dweller, but they are hunters through and through and require a lot of exercise. If you are in the market for a medium-size sporting breed and live in the suburbs or in a rural area, then the Brittany might be a good choice.

The smallest dog in the Sporting Group is the American Cocker. Just slightly larger, and easier to groom, is the English Cocker. This is a merry little dog, and provided you can give it some exercise, it is not too large to do well in an urban setting. There are two springer spaniels, English and Welsh. The English Springer is divided between show and hunting lines that are somewhat dissimilar in appearance. Dogs from hunting lines are likely to be smaller and have shorter ears. English Springers from show lines will usually need professional grooming. Welsh Springers are slightly smaller in size and not as popular a breed. The Irish Water Spaniel is a very trainable breed, about the size of a retriever. Its biggest disadvantage is its coat. This dog will need the services of a professional groomer.

THE HOUND GROUP

The hound breeds can be divided into scent and sight hounds. Scent hounds use their highly developed sense of smell to track their prey and lead their master to the quarry. Some breeds work individually, while others work in a pack. The sight hounds use their superior eyesight to find, chase, and then kill their prey. Because they mainly hunt in packs, hounds are generally not dog-aggressive. However, unlike the sporting breeds that were developed to work closely with man, hounds have a tendency to be independent and not take human direction readily. Many of the hound breeds are shorthaired and do not require much grooming maintenance.

Most hounds cannot be trusted off the leash. If you give a hound a chance to run loose, you may never see him again. Scent hounds often become oblivious to their owners' calls when on the track of an interesting scent. The sight hounds can spot a cat or a Poodle hundreds of yards away, and the chase is on. I knew one Saluki owner who lived in a rural area. On occasion her Saluki would escape from his kennel run and disappear. The owner would have to hire the local crop duster to go up in his plane to locate her dog. On one occasion he was spotted sixteen miles from his home. If your choice is one of the hound breeds, then a fenced yard is recommended, and all walks should be taken with your dog on leash, except perhaps with the popular Dachshund or a Basset Hound. These two hound breeds with their short legs cannot cover too much ground, and you may be able to turn them loose on a walk in a safe area where dogs are permitted to be off leash.

SCENT HOUNDS

Of the hound breeds, the Beagle and Dachshund are the two most popular members. The cartoon character Snoopy has immortalized the Beagle. Although a popular housedog, the Beagle continues to be used for hunting rabbits in many areas of the United States. The Dachshund, and here I am biased, is one of the more trainable of the hound breeds. At two dogs long and half a dog high, the Dachshund comes in two sizes, miniature—under eleven pounds—and standard, and has three coat varieties. The smooth-haired variety has a no-maintenance coat, the longhair has a coat similar to a setter, and the wirehaired variety has a coat like a terrier. With his ultra short-legs, the Dachshund requires little exercise, which makes him suitable for apartment dwelling and easy to exercise for senior citizens. The Dachshund has a deep bark, so it makes an excellent watchdog. It sounds like there is a German Shepherd on the other side of the door. Unfortunately, the Dachshund suffers from degenerative disc disease, which often causes paralysis. Disc disease is more prevalent in the standard than the miniature variety. With this knowledge of back problems, Dachshund owners must make an effort to keep their dogs trim and avoid unnecessary stair climbing.

If the Basset Hound had regular-length legs, he would be considered a large breed. Bassets tend to be lazy and do not require the exercise of many of the hounds. For this reason they can live comfortably in an urban setting. However, many Bassets are still used for hunting rabbits. If you want a dog that looks rather like a Basset then you might consider a PBGV. This is a dog with a long name, Petit Basset Griffon Vendeen, and long, wavy hair. It is a charming dog that looks more like a mutt than a purebred dog.

The Norwegian Elkhound was bred to hunt moose. The Elkhound is considerably different in appearance from the rest of the scent hounds. He has a coat more like that of a German

Shepherd Dog and sheds in like manner. While the rest of the scent hounds have drop ears, the Elkhound with his prick ears has a more intimidating look. Somehow, the Elkhound does not fit the stereotype of a scent hound, and you might expect to find him in the Working Group.

Many of the less popular scent hounds, like the Foxhound, are still used for hunting rather than kept as family pets. Some scent hounds "bay" rather than bark, and the noise they make can be very annoying to your neighbors.

SIGHT HOUNDS

Sight hounds are long-legged, graceful, and usually independent. Of all the sight hound breeds, the Whippet probably would make the best pet. They have very short coats, are medium-sized, and are not quite so independent as some of the other sight hounds. However, the Whippet does not handle the cold well and would be better suited to living in the southern part of the United States, where the temperatures do not stay below freezing for weeks at a time.

Greyhounds are similar in looks to the Whippet but considerably larger. Many Greyhounds start out their lives as "track" dogs rather than pets. They raise these unfortunate track dogs for one purpose only, to win Greyhound races. If they do not win, they become disposable. Fortunately, for some of these Greyhounds, luck is on their side, and people adopt them at the end of their racing careers. If you are looking for an older dog to rescue, then a Greyhound from the track might make a suitable pet for you. If you do decide to adopt a racing Greyhound, you will need to train it just like a little puppy. Therefore, turn to Chapter 19—"Taking Over Someone Else's Problem."

The Basenji, the smallest of the sight hounds, has a feline personality. If you own a Basenji be prepared to erect a tall fence, and have no tree limbs extending beyond its boundaries. Basenjis can climb and will scramble up a tree, walk out along a limb, and leave the yard in a manner similar to a cat. Basenjis are also feline in the way they groom themselves. They are sometimes called "the barkless dog," but this is a misnomer. While they do not bark, they yodel instead—an eerie sound that reminds you that their home of origin is darkest Africa!

The Afghan is probably one of the most elegant breeds, but its coat is almost impossible for the average pet owner to care for. His look of superiority goes along with an independent nature, which makes training challenging. If you like the look of the Afghan but do not want to spend several hours a week grooming your dog, you might want to consider owning a Saluki, a breed with a lot less hair. Another large, elegant breed with a long, wavy coat is the Borzoi.

The most popular sight hound is the Rhodesian Ridgeback, and of all the hound breeds, it is the most likely to make a personal protection dog. The breed was originally developed to hunt lions; so these dogs are courageous. Ridgebacks are large and intimidating with no-maintenance coats.

The largest of the hound breeds is the Irish Wolfhound, which stands more than thirty inches tall and weighs well over one hundred pounds. As the name implies, this breed was once used to hunt wolves. Surprisingly, the Wolfhound has a gentle nature, a necessary virtue considering his size. He has a rough, easy-to-care-for coat. Unfortunately, the Wolfhound is not long-lived just like many of the other giant breeds.

THE WORKING GROUP

Dogs in this group have been bred to serve man in many various ways. In this group you will find personal protection dogs, guard dogs, "image dogs," sled dogs, and rescue dogs. The breeds range in size from medium to giant. Giant breeds usually have a very short life span. For many dog owners, no matter how long their dogs live, they still die all too soon. The giant breeds often have half the life span of the average dog. It is difficult to lose a dog after twelve to fifteen years; they become members of the family. To buy a breed that you will lose after only six to seven years seems such a waste of emotions.

None of the breeds within this group makes a good urban/apartment dweller. Most of the working breeds require a considerable amount of exercise. The giant breeds, while not needing as much exercise, are too large to live in an apartment or small house. In addition, if you have to walk your giant dog in the park, you need to consider the amount of feces you will have to pick up. It can be a huge task!

If you select a breed known for its protective nature, you must be prepared to attend obedience classes and train your dog well beyond the basic level. Many protection breeds need to take a refresher obedience course several times throughout their lives. Most protection breeds are German in origin and have a tendency to be stubborn and hardheaded and need a firm hand. Many of the protection breeds are strong, powerful dogs that without proper socialization and training could become dangerous to own, particularly in an urban or suburban setting where dogs are required to live closely with other people and pets. Many dogs in this group are one-person or one-family dogs and do not like strangers entering their environment. This is all very well if you live alone, but if you have a family, this can be a difficult or even dangerous situation, particularly when children are involved. Protection breeds will protect their "children" from their children's friends. If your children bring friends home and you do not lock up the dog first, someone may end up getting bitten. Rough play between children may seem like an attack to your dog, and he may go into protection mode.

I mention "image dogs." The image breeds change over time. Some people want to own a dog that is perceived as a Rambo. One of the image dogs of today is the Rottweiler. In the past it was the Akita and before that the Doberman Pinscher. Sometimes the breed gets a bum rap as a dangerous dog, but sometimes there is some truth to the accusation. Some people buy an image breed to make a statement. Unfortunately, they do not take the time to train the dog, and get perverse delight out of the dog putting terror into the heart of all it meets. This type of owner is who so often gives the breed a bad name, not the breed itself.

The Rottweiler is the most popular dog in the Working Group, followed by the Boxer. The Rottweiler is so strong and powerful that it is too much dog for the average pet owner to handle. If you decide the Rottweiler is the breed for you, check first with your insurance company before you go looking for a puppy. Once you own a Rottweiler, many insurance companies fail to renew your household insurance. Your insurance company may even cancel your policy on the spot if it finds out this breed is living in your home. The Rottie has such powerful jaws that it can inflict serious damage should it bite someone.

The Boxer is a much smaller breed that is light on its feet. It uses its front legs and paws to "box," and the biggest complaint from Boxer owners is the way the dog uses its legs to paw at them. This is particularly true if the owner is trying to get the dog to do something it would prefer not to do. Another disadvantage with the Boxer is that the pushed-in face sometimes creates breathing difficulties, particularly in hot weather. Therefore, if you live in a hot and humid climate, this might not be the best choice for you, unless you plan on keeping the dog in the house when hot weather makes breathing difficult.

The Doberman Pinscher is another popular shorthaired dog, once at the height of popularity. Several years ago, people overbred the Doberman, and today the breed has many health problems that shorten its life. Before you buy a Doberman, talk to a veterinarian first before you fall in love with a puppy. This breed takes readily to obedience training.

The Giant Schnauzer is a large, intimidating breed that requires the services of a professional groomer. The tallest breed in the Working Group is the Great Dane. The Akita is a powerful dog whose facial expression rarely lets you know what he is thinking, and this makes training him difficult. He has a thick double coat, which will put great strain on your vacuum cleaner.

The Standard Schauzer is a medium-sized dog that will need professional grooming. If you once owned a Miniature Schnauzer and you have decided you want a similar but larger dog, the temperament of the Standard is nothing at all like that of the Miniature Schnauzer. The Standard Schnauzer is a working dog, while the Miniature is a terrier. The Standard Schnauzer is one of the more trainable breeds in the Working Group.

The guard dogs are really livestock protection dogs. They do not take to training as easily as the personal protection breeds. Rather than work alongside man, they were developed in Europe to live among the flocks of sheep and goats to protect them from predators. These breeds are light in color so they can blend in with the sheep and take the big bad wolf by surprise. If you want to own a livestock protection breed, you need a kennel run or an area where the dog can be securely confined when you have workmen or visiting friends or children in the house. Your family will take on the role of the dog's flock, but instead of protecting sheep he will protect you to the best of his ability, which may not always be appropriate!

The Great Pyrenees is the most popular of the guardian breeds. He is large and hairy and will need weekly brushing. He will probably require the services of a professional groomer, but you may not find one willing to take on a dog of that size.

Three sled dogs are found in the Working Group. If you enjoy vacuuming you will certainly get a workout! The most popular sled dog is the Siberian Husky. The wolflike appearances of both the Husky and the Alaskan Malamute appeal to many people. The Samoyed is all white and was once used as a herding dog. Sled dogs have been bred to run steadily over long distances, working alongside other dogs in a pack. For this reason, they are more difficult to train than the personal protection breeds that work individually with man. You cannot trust a sled dog off the leash, and you become their "musher" when you take them for a walk. It is difficult to teach a sled dog not to pull, so if taking walks with your dog is in your agenda, a sled dog would be a poor choice.

The rescue dogs are the Saint Bernard, Newfoundland, and Portuguese Water Dog. The Saint was used to find persons buried in snow in the Swiss Alps, while the Newfoundland was used to rescue drowning victims off the coast of Canada. These aforementioned dogs are giant breeds, weighing more than one hundred pounds. Their coats, unless you have a smooth-haired Saint Bernard, are as difficult to maintain as the Great Pyrenees. Finding a groomer willing to take all day to groom one of these dogs will be difficult. The medium-sized Portuguese was bred to take nets to fishermen and, in addition, take flotation devices to victims who had fallen into the water. The Portuguese is not a very serious breed and needs regular professional grooming as often as a Standard Poodle.

The Terrier Group

The terriers are mainly British breeds, once used to kill vermin. Many have a high energy level, but due to their medium to small size, they can get enough exercise racing around an apartment! If you have a fenced backyard, terriers take great delight in digging for imaginary rodents. One cold winter day, one of our clients found his furnace not working. When the gas company came out on a service call it was discovered that his terrier had dug up and ruptured the natural gas pipeline buried three feet under the ground. It cost him several hundred dollars to repair the damage done by his dog.

Terriers come in three types of coats, smooth, wire, and soft. Dogs with the wirehair coats usually require the services of a professional groomer, even though this may not be explained in books about the breed. The terriers with the soft coats need more professional grooming than the rest of the terriers, and their owners will need to maintain their coats between monthly visits to Canine Supercuts.

Most terriers have a devil-may-care attitude and do not take life very seriously. For this reason, they make amusing companions, although not very obedient pets. These dogs can be scrappy and often have a "Napoleon complex." As far as a terrier is concerned, no dog is too large to lick. Most terriers are robust dogs, and they are often a good choice for families with older children. The short-legged terriers do not need the exercise of the long-legged terriers and make a good choice of dog for seniors. Due to their genetic background, terriers have acute hearing and will bark at the slightest sound, so this could cause problems with your neighbors.

The Airedale is the king of terriers and continues to be used in Germany for police work. If you like the terrier look but want an intimidating dog, the Airedale might just be the dog for you. It is one of the easier terriers to teach to respond to basic obedience commands. If you like the look of the Airedale but do not want large a dog, you might consider the Welsh Terrier. However, you will not find a Welsh Terrier as easy to train as an Airedale.

The most popular terrier is the Miniature Schnauzer. It is probably the easiest of the terriers to train in basic obedience. They require professional grooming every couple of months. Schnauzers are the most vocal of the terriers. If a barking dog is annoying to you or would be annoying to your neighbors, then you should choose a different terrier breed to share your home for the next fourteen years or consider having the dog debarked.

Three short-legged terriers are next to the Miniature Schnauzer in popularity. These are the West Highland White Terrier, the Scottish Terrier, and the Cairn Terrier. None of these terriers thinks too highly of obedience training. However, they do make delightful companions if obeying obedience commands is not high on your list of priorities.

The Border Terrier is one of the least scrappy of the terriers and is one of the more trainable. The Jack Russell is about to become an AKC-registered breed. Jack Russells come in both smooth and rough coats and can be long- or short-legged. They have been popular for years with the horsy set. They are probably the most agile of the terriers and have no trouble scaling a six-foot fence.

Fox Terriers are small, long-legged terriers that come in wire and smooth coats. The Soft Coated Wheaton Terrier is a medium-sized dog that has a tendency to be hyperactive. His coat mats easily, so you must be prepared to visit the groomer more often than the owners of other terrier breeds.

The most powerful terrier is the American Staffordshire Terrier, or Pit Bull Terrier as he is often referred to. This breed has one of the worst reputations in the dog world. Bred for fighting, these dog are still used illegally for this purpose. Like the Rottweiler, owning an Am Staff can be reason for your insurance company to tell you to find another carrier. If you want to be ostracized by other dog owners, then consider owning this breed. They are an image dog like the Rottweiler and a breed often owned by members of the underworld. Many Am Staffs are sweet dogs, and people are attracted to their powerful looks. If you decide to own an Am Staff, be particularly careful in the selection of a breeder, and be sure to give your puppy extra socialization.

THE TOY GROUP

As we move into the twenty-first Century, we find at least seven toy breeds among the twenty most popular dogs registered with the American Kennel Club. For centuries, the toy breeds' only job has been to be a companion to man. Toy dogs are affectionate and intelligent, but they can also be manipulative. They know man dotes on them, and they tend to take advantage of that. A toy dog owner sometimes overlooks behavior not tolerated with a larger breed. Childless couples often favor toy breeds, and these dogs become their surrogate children. You can dress up a toy dog in a jacket and hat, and people think, "How cute." Do something like this with a Doberman, and people think you are weird.

Many of the dogs in the Toy Group have relatively easy-to-care-for coats. However, no matter the type of coat, most owners of toy breeds enjoy pampering their pets. Brushing and combing their tiny companions becomes therapeutic. Nevertheless, some members of the Toy Group do need to visit the dog groomer on a regular basis. Many toy breeds suffer from dental problems and often lose most of their teeth. Toy breeds are fragile and should not be in a home with young children.

There is one major training problem associated with toy breeds, and it is that of house soiling. Many toy breeds get in the habit of eliminating in the house. There is no physical reason for this. The size of the toy dog's bladder is in direct proportion to his size. Toy breeds eat and drink less than larger dogs, so there is no reason for their lack of bladder and bowel control. I believe the owner of the toy is directly responsible for many house-soiling problems. When a larger breed soils the house, it is immediately obvious, and the owner does something about it. When a toy dog soils the house, it is hardly noticeable until the house starts reeking of urine. By then, the habit is well-established. Moreover, owners of toy breeds often have difficulty correcting their dogs, which only adds to the problem.

The most popular toy breed listed is the Chihuahua, followed by the Yorkshire Terrier, Pomeranian, and Shih Tzu. It is likely that the Toy Poodle is actually the most popular toy breed. However, the three poodle varieties are all lumped together as one, so it is only speculation to say the Toy Poodle is top of the toy list. If that is the case, then there are eight toys among the top twenty most popular breeds.

Since most toys are affectionate and intelligent, there are not many considerations to help you choose between the breeds except for their looks. The Toy Poodle, Papillon, and Pomeranian are probably the three easiest toys to train in basic obedience commands. There are several toy breeds that have pushed-in faces, which often makes breathing difficult for them. When the weather is hot, you must make sure these dogs, like the Boxer, do not get overheated.

THE NON-SPORTING GROUP

Dog are placed within this group when they are so far removed from their original purpose that they do not fit into any other categories. You might expect to find a number of breeds from this group in the Toy Group, except these dogs are just slightly larger in stature than the toys. Temperaments in the Non-sporting Group range from friendly and affectionate to dominant and difficult, but many dogs in this group take readily to training. Coats vary from no maintenance to high maintenance that requires professional grooming.

Poodles are the most popular dogs in the Non-sporting Group, though strangely enough, the Poodle was once used for hunting in Germany. Many Poodles still have the instinct to flush quail and pheasant. Poodles require regular professional grooming. They are one of the most intelligent of all breeds and accept training very well.

The Boston Terrier is the second most popular member of this group. The Boston is an all-American dog and a highly athletic one at that. The Bulldog is also a popular member of the Non-sporting Group. Like the Doberman, the Bulldog has a myriad of health problems. If you are considering adding this breed to your household, be sure to talk to a veterinarian before you start looking for a puppy. You might well change your mind once you hear about all the problems you might be facing as the owner of a Bulldog. Except for the intervention of a veterinarian, this breed would be all but extinct. The Bulldog cannot breed or whelp without human interference.

The Bichon Frise is a charming, small, fluffy white dog that requires a lot of maintenance between grooming appointments. The Lhasa Apso looks very much like its cousin, the Shih Tzu, but does not have its sweet disposition. The Dalmatian is one of the largest dogs in the Non-sporting Group. Dalmatians have nice short coats and are relatively easy to train. If you decide to get a Dalmatian, be sure to check that the puppy you choose does not have a hearing problem. This breed is plagued with deafness problems. Be careful that you do not take a puppy home with you, fall in love with it, and then later discover it is deaf. Should this happen, you will have to train the dog using hand signals. While it is possible to train a dog this way, it is not as easy as with verbal cues. If you are looking at a litter of Dalmatians, take one puppy at a time away from the litter. Then when the puppy is not looking at you, bang two metal pie pans together. Watch the puppy's reaction when you do this. If he does not react to the noise, there is a good chance he may be deaf, and you should select a different puppy.

The most appealing-looking puppy in the Non-sporting Group is the Chow Chow. However, this cute puppy often turns into a difficult adult dog with anyone but his immediate family. The Chow's coat is the most difficult to groom of this group, and many grooming shops refuse to touch this breed. This leaves the owner with a monumental chore. The Chow, with his furry face, is a difficult dog to read, and training him is not easy.

THE HERDING GROUP

Dogs in this group are some of the most intelligent breeds there are. While you might think owning a very smart dog is a wise choice, smart dogs can think of more ways to get into trouble than dogs of average intelligence. Many of the breeds in the Herding Group have high energy levels and are only a couple of generations removed from total working dogs. Dogs with intelligence and high energy need a job to do to keep them out of trouble. For this reason, only consider a dog from this group if you are prepared to spend time exercising and working with your dog. Many of these breeds excel in obedience, agility, or herding.

Dogs in the Herding Group are often notorious barkers. They have excellent eyesight and will bark at anything that moves. Herding breeds need to be confined behind a fence. Many herding dogs wind up as highway statistics because they will chase any vehicle going along the road if they can possibly reach it. They will also herd children on skateboards and bicycles, and when the child does not turn in the direction the dog wants, he does what he would do with recalcitrant livestock—he nips to make the child "mind." If you choose a herding breed, you will need to pay particular attention to what your dog is up to if he is out playing with children. Nipping is part of life for a herding dog. They do not discriminate between children, sheep, or cattle.

Coats of the herding breeds range from no maintenance (the Australian Cattle Dog) to major maintenance (the Bearded Collie and the Old English Sheepdog). Many of the coats of the herding breeds are double coats: a soft, downy undercoat intermixed with longer hair. These coats protect the dog from inclement weather when he is working out on the farm, and they end up on your carpet during the twice-yearly shedding season.

The most popular dog in the Herding Group is the German Shepherd Dog. Most people think of this dog as a personal protection, or police, dog but at one time the German Shepherd was a herding dog. Thus, he is placed in this group. The German Shepherd you often see today is not the Rin Tin Tin of yesteryear. You can split the German Shepherd into two types: the "American" shepherd, which is often nervous and has poor physique, and the "German-style" shepherd, which is the type used by law enforcement officers. The "German-style" shepherd has a lot of drive and will need more training than the "American-style" shepherd. Both these varieties of German Shepherd are notorious barkers.

The three Belgian shepherd dogs are another breed you might associate with police work, but they, too, remain in the Herding Group. All three varieties are easy to train and make good family companions. The Belgian Malinois is the only variety with short hair, and is the most popular of the Belgian shepherd varieties with law enforcement officers. It is an outstanding breed used for drug detection and apprehending criminals.

Another popular member of the Herding Group is the Shetland Sheepdog, often incorrectly referred to as the Miniature Collie. The maximum size for a Sheltie is sixteen inches, although some of these dogs do get larger than that. Shelties are one of the easiest dogs to train and, because of their small size, live happily in suburbia. They make excellent family dogs and will listen to commands from the children once they have been properly obedience-trained. Like many of the herding breeds, Shelties are notorious barkers. Another small herding dog is the Welsh Corgi, which comes in two flavors: Cardigan (with a tail) and Pembroke (without a tail). Corgis, with their short legs, may be the only members of this group that might adapt to apartment living. A large number of Corgis live in the Queen's apartment at Buckingham Palace, but this apartment is larger than what most of us consider an apartment to be!

The premier herding dog is the Border Collie, recently accepted for registration by the American Kennel Club. This was an unpopular decision forced on the herding community, and many Border Collies in the United States still continue to be registered by one of the independent Border Collie registries instead of the AKC. For this reason, the Border Collie is a much more popular breed than AKC statistics show. Many Border Collies want to do only one thing, work! For this reason they do not do well in urban living and are happiest when they have a large fenced-in area in which to run and some chore to do, whether it is obedience, herding, or agility. Most Border Collies have a wash-and-wear coat.

The Australian Shepherd is similar to the Border Collie, only it has no tail. This breed is much more vocal than a Border Collie and usually has a heavier coat, which requires more grooming. Many Aussies have attractive merle coloring. Another once-popular breed is the Lassie-type Collie once known for its high intelligence. Unfortunately this is no longer the case, and their coats require considerable grooming. If you once dreamed about owning Lassie, consider a Shetland Sheepdog instead.

The Old English Sheepdog and the Bearded Collie have coats that require daily attention. Out herding, both of these breeds would become tangled in a briar patch on their way to gather the sheep and would never be seen again. The Beardie, also a notorious barker, has a clownish character, so he does not take work very seriously.

Australian Cattle Dogs are easy to care for. Bred to work cattle rather than sheep, this breed is physically and mentally tougher than most of the other herding dogs. Because cows are much more physically challenging to herd than sheep, they require a mentally and physically tougher dog to handle them.

If none of these breeds or groups of dogs appeals to you, then you may wish to consider a "rare" breed or a mix. Rare breeds often have their own set of genetic problems and temperaments. They are likely to have a small gene pool, which may lead to hereditary problems. If you acquire a mixed-breed, you can only guess what you are getting. If that is your choice, visit the local shelter and adopt a dog from there. There are not enough homes for dogs in the shelters. If you adopt a shelter dog, take time to read Chapter 19, "Taking Over Someone Else's Problem."

CHAPTER 4

Playing Detective

Do not believe everything you read in print. We are reminded of that from time to time. When you want more details about the breeds that interest you, one of your best sources is a book on that particular breed. Remember that the author of a book on a specific breed is often wearing rose-colored glasses, which sometime clouds her vision. The breed's good points are often emphasized, while the bad are sometimes glossed over.

Many of the details found in breed books will be important to your selection. The size of the dog and exercise requirements most likely are pretty accurate. However, when it comes to training or grooming, what one person might consider easy another might find difficult. So, once you have narrowed down your choices, read

◀ You can find information about different breeds of dogs on the World Wide Web. *Photo by Margret Taylor. Dachshund, Hound Group.*

a book on the individual breed and then do some detective work of your own. It will pay dividends in the end.

Four different pet care professionals should be able to give you a reasonably unbiased assessment of the breeds that interest you. Be prepared to offer to pay them for their time. They probably will not charge you, but it would be fair to make the offer.

A VETERINARIAN

Veterinarians meet hundreds of dogs each year, some for routine inoculations and others for minor to serious health problems. Veterinarians are often well-acquainted with the genetic defects in many of the different breeds of dogs, either through personal contact or through articles published in the *Journal of the American Veterinary Medical Association*. This journal also discusses temperament problems associated with different breeds. It is sometimes understandable if a sick or injured dog bites the vet, but what about the dog that goes in for a routine inoculation and terrorizes the doctor and his staff? Certain breeds have a reputation as being difficult to handle when they visit the animal hospital, and these same breeds are likely to be antagonistic in other situations as well.

Call an animal hospital, talk to the staff members, and tell them what breeds or mixes you are considering. They can tell you if you are making a wise choice. They may say you are considering a breed that is hard to handle or that has health issues not mentioned in the book you just read. One vet who used to attend to our dogs had a skull-and-crossbones stamp that he placed on the file of any dog that gave him trouble. This was his way of warning his staff in advance that a particular dog would need special handling.

A DOG TRAINER

Dog trainers are often the last resort in the battle to control "Capone" before the owner gives up the fight, and also the dog. However, many dogs using the services of a dog trainer are not problem dogs at all. Responsible owners take their dogs to training class to teach them some manners before things get out of control.

A dog trainer can give you insight as to the trainability and temperament of many different breeds. Choose a trainer who handles pet dogs as opposed to a personal protection trainer, who deals with the more assertive breeds. You might ask if it is possible to attend a training class so that you can see for yourself the way different breeds react during the training process. If there are breeds enrolled that interest you, you might be able to talk to these dogs' owners and find out firsthand how easy the breed is for the average owner to live with. Most dog owners like to talk about their dogs and expand on their good points and their problem areas. A dog trainer can tell you if the breed you are considering is easy to house-train and whether it barks excessively. You will learn if it has a tendency to be assertive with other dogs and if it is a challenge to train to respond to basic commands. Some breeds are fast learners, some appear mentally challenged, and others do not even care to learn. The old adage "All dogs want to please their owners" is not necessarily true for all dogs!

A DOG GROOMER

Tell dog groomers what breed you are considering, and they will tell you just how easy or difficult the coat will be to care for. Dog books often fail to mention the hours required to groom the coats of certain breeds or that the dog's coat needs to be clipped every six weeks. Some books gloss over the fact that the breed being described within its pages needs regular professional grooming. The cost to have a dog professionally groomed often comes as a shock to the owner when taking the dog to Canine Supercuts for his first visit. Many breeds need to visit the groomer between six and eight times a year. That can add up to well over $200, without even including the tip! Yes, you do tip the groomer as you would the barber or your beautician. The time to consider whether you can afford this service is before you buy the dog.

People who choose a "coated" breed, like a Poodle, Bichon Frise, or Lhasa Apso, often choose the breed for the way it looks rather than for the way the dog is most likely to behave. However, these breeds and others like them only look the way they do in pictures because of regular brushing or clipping. Few owners have the expertise or time to clip a Poodle or Bichon or comb out a Lhasa. In addition, owners of dogs with difficult coats must find time to maintain the coat between grooming appointments, which for some breeds means daily combing or brushing.

Some breeds do not take kindly to being handled by a groomer, and when the dog acts up, many grooming salons add combat fees to the basic price charged for their service. A dog groomer can tell you which breeds have sweet and cooperative personalities and which breeds they would prefer to send to their competitor. Some grooming shops even refuse to take certain breeds, and if that is the case with the breed you have selected you may well end up having to do the grooming yourself. This will not matter if your breed is shorthaired, but if your dog has a heavy coat you may wish you had chosen some other breed.

A KENNEL OWNER

Like the other pet professionals, a kennel owner will come into daily contact with many different breeds over a year's time. Some breeds enjoy going to a kennel because they are social toward other dogs. Other breeds are very owner-dependent and sit in the corner of their run and sulk, or try to escape at every opportunity. Some dogs will challenge anyone and any dog walking past their run, creating an atmosphere of apprehension.

Kennel owners will be able to tell you if the breed you are considering is easy to handle and cooperative with strangers. They will know which breeds are generally fear-biters and which are dirty when it comes to house soiling. If you own a breed that is difficult to board, the kennel may be full when you call up to book space for your dog while you go on vacation. The conversation may go something like this:

Kennel staff: "Hello, Holidog Inn. May I help you?"

Dog owner: "I'd like to arrange to board my dog for the next two weeks."

Kennel staff: "Certainly, sir. What breed of dog do you have?"

Dog owner: "A Grumblehound."

Kennel staff: "Errrr, just let me check and see what we have available." (long pause) "Oh, I'm sorry, sir, but we are all booked up for that period of time. Why don't you call Take Anydog Kennel? I'm sure they will have space. Goodbye."

Those of us in the pet care industry are sometimes biased when it comes to how we feel about certain breeds. Perhaps we have had a particularly bad experience with one member of a breed that has since clouded our dealings with all others. However, when you talk to the pet professionals about the breed you have in mind, you may get a similar report from all of them. If the report is bad, you would be wise to take notice. With luck you will have selected a breed about which they only have nice things to say.

CHAPTER 5

Going to the Right Source

Now that you have decided on the breed of dog with which you would like to share your life, it is time to locate a puppy. Choosing the right breeder will be a big step in selecting a healthy, well-adjusted puppy. (See Chapter 18, "The Patter of Tiny Paws.") Some of the first people to ask for recommendations for a breeder are those same pet care professionals who helped you make your decision as to which breed would best suit you. If you are thinking of a purebred puppy, you can contact the American Kennel Club or the United Kennel Club for the name of a local or national breed club. Most of these clubs offer a breeder referral program. If you know someone who owns the breed you would like to own, ask that person for recommendations as to where you could find a dog of the same breed. Occasionally someone might have an advertise-

◀ It is not a good idea to buy two puppies at the same time. They will bond to each other, rather than to you. *Photo by Margret Taylor. Australian Shepherds, Herding Group.*

ment in the local paper. You can also check the classified section of
the monthly dog magazines. If you go that route, you may be buying a puppy sight unseen.

BUYING A PUPPY LOCALLY

If you go to look at a litter of puppies, pay attention to the way
they are being housed and raised. Are the facilities clean? Do the
puppies have access to the outside so they can eliminate away from
the nest? A puppy raised in a clean environment will be much easier to housebreak than one kept in a small, dirty pen. Are the puppies' parents available? If the bitch was bred to an outside stud, you
will not be able to meet the sire, but the mother of the puppies
should be on the premises. Is she friendly? Occasionally a bitch is
very protective around her puppies, but by the time the puppies are
seven weeks old, they should be weaned, and the mother should
pay little attention to them. Ask the breeder if the puppies have
been handled by several different people and children. Early socialization is all-important for a well-adjusted puppy.

Is the breeder able to produce OFA and CERF certificates? (See
Chapter 18.) Do not take the breeder's word that the parents have
an OFA or CERF number; ask to see the certificates. Are the puppies registered? Is the litter registration certificate available? Have
the puppies received any inoculations? Has the breeder had the litter checked for worms? Has the breeder's veterinarian examined
them? If the puppies are not yet old enough to leave the breeder's
home, then it is unlikely that they will have received a health check.
Find out if a veterinarian will examine the puppies when they are
old enough to leave for their new homes. In addition, does the
breeder guarantee the health of the puppy?

What is the puppy being fed? The breeder should be feeding a
top-quality dog food. Unfortunately, some breeders feed the
cheapest dry dog food available. If this is the case, the puppy will
be off to a poor start. Does the breeder show interest in you, or
only in your checkbook?

At what age will the breeder release the puppy to his new home? A puppy should remain with his mother and littermates until he is seven weeks old. By remaining with the litter until then, a puppy will receive the proper canine training. A mother dog will discipline her puppies for misbehavior if they bite too hard on a teat or pull on her tail. A littermate will tell off a sibling if one puppy bites down too hard on another. A breeder who tries to sell you a puppy of less than six weeks of age is a breeder of whom to stay clear. This type of breeder is only looking at the bottom line. By releasing a puppy at an early age, the breeder saves on dog food, shots, and work. Occasionally, if you are facing a three-day weekend at the time the puppies reach six and one-half weeks, you might be allowed to take a puppy home a few days early. It is always good to bring home a puppy over a long weekend, when you will have more time to get acquainted with each other.

Occasionally you may find that a breeder has been unable to sell some or all of the puppies at the optimum age of seven weeks. If puppies remain with their littermates for too long, they become dog-oriented, rather than people-oriented. If you look at a litter of puppies older than nine weeks of age, try to find out if each puppy has been given adequate individual socialization with humans.

Understandably, breeders of toy dogs are often reluctant to let their charges leave much before three months of age. Toy puppies are so tiny that many breeders want to keep them until they are a little bigger and less vulnerable to being stepped on. The breeder of a toy dog who has kept the puppies past nine weeks of age will most likely have handled and socialized with them. After all, toy dogs are born to much smaller litters so that individual attention is easy to give.

One piece of advice I give all parents who are going to look at a litter of puppies is this: Leave your children at home while you go puppy shopping! You may not like what you see when you visit the litter. However, if the children are along they may persuade you to take a puppy against your better judgment. Rather than listen to the crying of a child who cannot understand why a puppy is not going home with him, the parent often buys a dog that will not make a suitable pet. Leave your children at home, and then if you are satisfied with the puppies in the litter you can always go home, collect your child, and take him along to help select Einstein—that is, provided the breeder gives you a choice of puppies.

Do not be surprised if the breeder is as interested in you and your lifestyle as you are in the breeder. Expect to be asked if you have a fenced backyard. Depending on the breed you choose, many breeders will not consider selling one of their puppies to someone without a fenced yard. The breeder may inquire about your working conditions, what you do for recreation, the ages of your children, and whether you have any other pets. You may be asked about former dog ownership. If you have owned dogs in the past, particularly if your previous dog died of old age, you are more likely to be offered a puppy than if you have a history of canine abandonment. A breeder who questions your reasons for wanting one of her puppies is showing that she cares about what happens to the puppies she has helped to bring into this world.

Some breeders select a puppy for you instead of letting you choose. There is nothing wrong with that. A breeder is likely to be a lot more experienced in puppy selection than you are. Therefore, do not be surprised if you are told which puppy is yours without you having much say in the matter.

PICKING A PUPPY

If you are offered a choice of puppies, you should observe the following. The puppy that knocks all the other puppies in the litter out of the way to get to you may end up being a pushy, dominant dog. A puppy that sits off to the side, all by itself, may be shy or independent. Ask the breeder if you may take each puppy that is available to a quiet location away from its littermates, where you can interact with each one individually. Place the puppy on the ground, and then walk away from him. Does he follow you? Does he just sit there? Does he get underfoot? Ideally, the puppy will follow along beside you as you walk about. If he starts grabbing your pant legs, he may be a dominant puppy. If the puppy just sits there without interacting, the puppy may be shy or independent. Call the puppy to you. How does he respond? If he comes right away, this is a good sign. If he jumps all over you once he reaches you, tearing at your clothing, he may be dominant. Pick up the puppy. Does he struggle or snuggle? A snuggler is likely to be an easier dog to train. Is he a licker? Dominant dogs rarely lick. Licking is a sign of submission. Turn him over on his back and lay him on the ground. If he struggles frantically for half a minute, he is probably dominant. If at first he struggles and then settles, he will be easier to handle.

Bring a couple of different toys along. Try throwing one out and see if the puppy retrieves. If he runs out and picks up the toy and then returns the toy to you, he is going to be an easy dog to work with. Some breeds are not natural retrievers, so this test will not work for all puppies. If possible, leave the puppy on his own for a short time and observe what he does. Does he bark and scream, or does he go off and investigate his surroundings? A puppy that becomes frantic when left alone may have social isolation problems down the road. The final test is to give him that marrowbone you cooked at home. (Turn to Chapter 7, "The Puppy Starter Kit.") Give the puppy a chance to gnaw on it for a few seconds, and then try to take it away from him. If he says, "All right, Boss, it's all yours," you have a subordinate puppy. However, if he growls at you, consider seriously whether this would be a good choice of puppy, particularly if you have children at home. One day, if this puppy steals one of their toys, he may bite your child while he tries to reclaim it.

Dominant, or alpha, puppies will be a lot harder to train than subordinate puppies. As adult dogs, they will try to be the pack leaders if given the chance. If you choose an alpha puppy, you will continuously have to impress upon him who is the leader of the pack. An alpha dog may submit to you, but he may not submit to other members of the pack, your family members.

ARE TWO BETTER THAN ONE?

When confronted with a litter of puppies, it may be hard to decide between two puppies, and you may be tempted to take two home with you. What a mistake that would be! Most breeders will not sanction such an idea, but sometimes if a breeder is having difficulty selling his puppies, he may suggest this concept to you. Finding the time to raise one puppy is often difficult. Raising two puppies is much more time consuming than just raising one. You may think it would be a good idea for Einstein to have a friend to keep him company all day, but two puppies get into more than twice the trouble of one. While you are supervising the house-training of one puppy, the other is piddling on the rug someplace else. Puppies will bond with whomever they spend most of their time, and that will not be with you! Do not lose sight of the fact that you are buying a puppy for your own companionship.

BUYING A PUPPY LONG-DISTANCE

Sometimes the breed you want to own is not available locally, and you may have to buy a puppy long-distance. This is not as unusual as it might sound. Well-known breeders ship their puppies to homes all over the country.

If you deal long-distance with a breeder, you will have to hope the puppy has been properly socialized and that he has been raised under clean conditions. You should expect to receive copies of the parents' OFA and CERF certificates, a pedigree, and pictures before the puppy is shipped to you. Alternatively, you may wish to fly or drive to the breeder's location to see the litter and collect your puppy. Breeders who sell long-distance are often well-known in their breed and are experienced in puppy selection. These breeders will usually supply you with references so that you can call owners of puppies from previous litters to see how satisfied they are with the puppies and with their dealings with the breeder.

One thing you should ask any breeder is whether you could return the puppy should something happen that forces you to give up the dog. Certainly, you have no plans in the future to find another home for Einstein, but sometimes life deals you an unexpected blow. One day you may be forced to place your dog in a new home. A reputable breeder should be willing to help a puppy buyer place the dog if circumstances change and the owner can no longer look after the dog. In fact, many breeders require that you give them first refusal should you ever need to place your dog in another home.

BUYING A PUPPY AT A PET STORE

Finally, how about buying a puppy from a pet store, one that carries puppies and kittens as part of its merchandise? No reputable breeder will sell a puppy to a pet store. Pet store puppies are usually raised under deplorable conditions and have been shipped cross-country to reach the stores in the malls. Many of these puppies are not even the breed listed on their registration papers. The parents of these pet store puppies have had none of the health checks mentioned earlier in this book. Additionally, these puppies have received little or no human socialization. Prices charged for puppies sold in pet stores are likely to be just as high, if not higher, than what you might expect to pay for a puppy bought from a reputable breeder. If you are in the market for a dog, never visit a pet store that offers puppies for sale. You might be tempted to buy a puppy on impulse. If you do, you are likely to be in for a great deal of heartache. Pet stores rely on impulse buyers to move their merchandise, so do not put temptation in your way by visiting one of these stores unless Einstein is already in residence and you are no longer puppy shopping.

Even if the breeder of your puppy has taken him for a health check, you should consider taking him to see a veterinarian of your choice, just to make sure there is nothing wrong with him. If you acquired a puppy that has not received a health check, you should definitely take him in for one. You do not want to bring a puppy into your home and then discover he has a health problem requiring you to return him to the breeder. This can cause a lot of heartache, particularly if there are children involved.

CHAPTER 6

Choosing
Dr. Doolittle

SELECTING A VET FOR EINSTEIN

Unless you already have a veterinarian, one you have perhaps used with previous pets, now is the time to select one with whom you will feel comfortable. I am sure we would all like to find a James Herriot, but since that is out of the question you need to think seriously about which animal hospital to use.

One of the most important considerations is if the animal hospital has an emergency service. Due to Murphy's Law, it seems as though you always need a vet in the middle of the night or on weekends. A practice that has more than one vet is more likely to have 24-hour emergency service than one that does not. Some sin-

◀ Until your puppy is older, when you take him to the vet for a checkup and his shots, do not allow him to walk on the floor unless he is too large to carry and hold on your lap. This will ensure that he will not pick up diseases he is not fully vaccinated against. *Photo by Kohler Photography. Cocker Spaniels, Sporting Group.*

gle-doctor hospitals team up with others in the area to form an emergency referral service. This form of service allows you access to veterinary care in an emergency. However, unless you are familiar with the area to which you have to go, you may have difficulty finding the hospital in the middle of the night. This will be particularly true during an emergency because you will be paying more attention to your dog than to where you are going. It is always easier to go to the animal hospital you are used to using.

In many of the larger cities, there are state-of-the-art emergency animal hospitals. Many of these hospitals are excellent, but the prices charged for their services are likely to be considerably higher than what you would expect to pay at your own vet's hospital after hours. In addition, they will have no records on your dog and may have to duplicate tests you have already paid for at your own veterinary hospital.

If you live in a suburban or urban area, most veterinarians' practices will be devoted to small animal care. However, if you live in a more rural setting you may need to choose between a "horse doctor" and a vet! Practices in rural areas are often split between large and small animals, and you would be wise to find out the focus of the practice. Doctors who treat large animals often have to leave for hours at a time, and unless there is another doctor on staff who just treats pets, you may not find anyone around if you suddenly have an emergency. Therefore, check to see the status of the practice if the vet looks after horses, sheep, and cows.

Today, many animal hospitals operate on an appointment-only basis, and for most clients this is the preferred way to see the vet.

Just like a human doctor, emergencies occasionally happen where the vet may be unavoidably delayed, but making an appointment for Einstein is preferable to sitting in the waiting room for hours, waiting your turn. In the larger cities, it is not uncommon for one veterinarian to own several animal hospitals. If you cannot get an appointment at one, you may be able to get into one of the other hospitals. They usually have one data base, so your records would be readily available at any of the hospitals in the group. This would also hold true for emergency treatment. One hospital out of the group may be designated as the emergency clinic.

Until he is older, when you do take your puppy to the vet for a checkup and his shots, do not allow him to walk on the floor unless he is too large to carry and hold on your lap. Although the hospital is likely to have been sanitized, you never know what the other clients might have tracked in that day in the way of disease. When I am taking a puppy to visit the vet, I always call ahead and ask the receptionist if there has been a case of Parvo virus in the hospital that day. If so, I change my appointment rather than expose my puppy to that disease.

A veterinarian should take time to talk to you while he is checking over Einstein. The front office staff should be friendly and helpful, and the hospital should smell clean. If you ever get bad vibes about a doctor, listen to your inner voice and change hospitals if there is another you can go to. Next to you, your veterinarian will be Einstein's best friend. Do not wait until it is too late to find out that you have chosen a vet unwisely.

Today, a number of veterinarians specialize, rather than being in general practice. The average dog owner does not realize this, but it is useful information to have. Occasionally, a dog will not respond to treatment. However, some veterinarians are reluctant to send you to an expert in the field. They may not want to admit they are stumped, or perhaps they do not feel that you can afford the services of an expert, which are likely to be much higher than what you are used to paying. As far as I am concerned, if I do not see results from the treatment before too much time has passed, I will ask to be referred to a specialist. There are veterinary cardiologists, ophthalmologists, allergists, orthopedic specialists, and doctors of internal medicine, the list goes on and on. If you are not satisfied with the results of the treatment your veterinarian has prescribed, then ask him if he will refer you to a specialist. Maybe all you need to do is seek a second opinion from another general practitioner, just as you might if you were dissatisfied with results from a human doctor. An alternative for some owners would be to consult with a school of veterinary medicine. These teaching hospitals are always in need of patients so that their students have training in many areas of animal medicine. However, these hospitals are not even in every state, much less in most people's local area. The advantages of a veterinary school over many local animal hospitals are that they have the most up-to-date equipment and the instructors have the latest techniques at their fingertips.

PILLING EINSTEIN MADE EASY

There will come a time when you will need to give Einstein a pill. This is not always as simple as it sounds. Some puppies object to anyone opening their mouths and will clamp their teeth together.

Others will allow you to open their mouths but then will squirm around, making it impossible to put a pill down their throats. Unless your puppy is too sick to eat, give him the pill in peanut butter. The pill will stick to the peanut butter, which will stick to the inside of your puppy's mouth. Dogs seem to like the taste of peanut butter and will willingly take a dollop off your finger. The peanut butter will hide the pill, and once it is in his mouth, Einstein will find it impossible to spit out and should end up swallowing it.

CHAPTER 7

The Puppy Starter Kit

Unless you have bought a puppy on impulse, you should prepare for Einstein's arrival in advance. Owning the right equipment and toys will mean the difference between success and frustration during those first transitional days, as he becomes accustomed to his new home. Many puppy owners are like new parents. They buy far more items than they need for the new arrival. Many of these things are quite unnecessary. The money they cost would be better spent on education! You can always add luxuries down the road when you know what Einstein needs.

◀ If you give a puppy too many toys, he will never learn what items in your house belong to him and what belongs to you. *Photo by Margret Taylor. Dachshund, Hound Group.*

ESSENTIAL ITEMS FOR EINSTEIN

DOG FOOD

Continue to feed Einstein the food he is used to eating. Dogs are not human and do not need to eat a variety of foods. It will only upset Einstein's digestive system if you constantly change his diet. Some people buy whatever brand is on sale. This may save you a few dollars initially. However, you may also end up with a large bill if Einstein suffers from a gastric upset and has to visit the vet. One reason to change Einstein's diet would be if he came from a shelter. Most shelters are unlikely to be able to afford to feed a high-quality dog food. For whatever reason you decide to switch food, do so gradually over several days. The higher the quality of the dog food, the better your dog can absorb the ingredients. The greater the amount of food absorbed by your dog, the less waste comes out, making cleaning up after him easier for you. Although premium dog food costs more to buy initially, you will not have to feed as much per serving as you would a cheaper brand. Therefore, the difference in overall cost is likely to be negligible. Remember that as Einstein grows, you will need to increase the amount of food he is consuming. Most puppies need to eat three meals a day until they are at least three months old. However, the midday meal might be hard to arrange if you are at work all day and there is nobody attending to Einstein. If that is the case, either leave food down all the time, termed a self-feeding schedule, or only feed him twice a day. Scheduled mealtimes make it easier to housebreak your dog. In addition, you can tell instantly if Einstein is off his feed. When a puppy quits eating, that is a good indication that something is amiss, but when a dog is on a self-feeding program, you may not realize that anything is wrong for several days. Once Einstein reaches his full growth, then cut back on the amount you are feeding him. Many dogs are overweight, just like humans, because they are overfed.

There is a movement afoot to go back to feeding dogs a natural diet. While there is nothing wrong with this, the average pet owner does not have time to prepare a special diet for her dog. Therefore, if your puppy comes from a breeder who feeds a natural diet and if you do not wish to continue this regime, switch Einstein over slowly to a commercial diet. If you are unsure of what to feed your puppy then consult your veterinarian.

A CRATE OR, IF YOU PREFER, AN INDOOR KENNEL

Most dog trainers, and educated dog owners, will tell you that a crate is one of the most important items you will ever own. Dogs are den animals that seek out small, dark places in which to bed down. A crate is your dog's den. Another way of looking at it is that the crate is Einstein's home within your home, rather like giving a child his own room. You will use the crate to confine Einstein whenever you cannot supervise him and also at night. You never use a crate for punishment. Crates come in various sizes and are made from different materials. The most popular are either fashioned out of plastic, with a metal grill door, or made entirely out of wire mesh. Wire crates give a dog more ventilation, which is useful if you live in a warm climate. Plastic crates give a dog a greater feeling of security. It would be best to purchase a crate that will be large enough to house Einstein when he is full-grown. You will need to confine Einstein to his crate for many months before you can trust him to be loose while you are gone. You can make a crate smaller in the beginning by adding a partition, but the only way to make it larger would be to buy a new one, an unnecessary expense if you already own a crate.

AN EXERCISE PEN IN ADDITION TO A CRATE

If Einstein has to be left indoors at home for hours at a time while you are gone, an exercise pen will be less restricting than a crate. Be sure it is tall enough so that Einstein cannot climb out of it, or buy a top to cover it so that it is more like a large crate. An ex-pen is freestanding, and usually made up of eight 2-foot panels. You can fold the pen to transport it from room to room or to take it outdoors. If you do not have a fenced yard, you may use an ex-pen as a temporary run or for the outside potty area. When you use the pen outside remember that it is not as secure as a fence; therefore you should consider anchoring it to the ground with stakes. Einstein should never be left outside in the ex-pen when you leave the house, and even when you are home you should check on him regularly.

A RETRACTABLE LEASH

If you take Einstein on walks around the neighborhood or to the park, a retractable leash is a great training tool. There are several brands on the market, but for our purposes we will sometimes call this type of leash a Flexi® since this is the brand name of the first well-known retractable leash on the market. A retractable leash gives Einstein more freedom than a regular leash. You can lock the leash to any length for up-close walking or allow Einstein the full length of the leash where there is room to let him stretch his legs. Many parks have a policy that requires a dog to be on leash. However, they often do not say how long the leash must be! Retractable leashes come in several lengths and weights. Buy the longest one available. A heavy-duty one is available for very large dogs. A retractable leash is one of the best ways to teach a puppy to come when called.

A BUCKLE OR SEMI-SLIP COLLAR

A puppy is much too young to wear a choke chain, or slip collar. These collars can actually choke a dog when used incorrectly. They can also snag on some object inside or outside your house and strangle your puppy. A buckle or plastic snap collar is safe because it cannot tighten at all. However, if it is too loose around the neck a puppy might be able to slip out of it, possibly getting away from you and getting injured in the process. In my opinion, a semi-slip collar is the safest for a puppy to wear. It will tighten a couple of inches when you exert pressure on the leash, but it cannot tighten enough to choke a dog. If your puppy gets frightened and tries to back away from something or somebody when out for a walk, a semi-slip collar will tighten just enough to prevent him from slipping out of it. When you buy Einstein's first collar, select an inexpensive one. He will outgrow several before he is full-grown.

A BELL

Purchase a small bell to attach to Einstein's collar. Puppies like to sneak off and get into trouble in areas of the house or yard where you do not want them to go. The ringing of the bell will alert you to the location of your puppy if he disappears from your sight. This is particularly useful at night when you take Einstein out in the yard to relieve himself before you put him to bed. Although you may not be able to see him in the dark, you will be able to hear where he is.

DOG TAG, OR ID

Although you plan on keeping in constant contact with Einstein, sometimes a puppy does get away from the owner. It is always a good idea for a dog to wear a tag attached to his collar, bearing the name, address, and phone number of the owner. Do not put your dog's name on the collar. If he somehow wanders off, you do not want him to respond to someone else's call. As another means of identification, when you go in for a checkup, your veterinarian can microchip Einstein.

FOOD BOWL, WATER BOWL, AND BUCKET

Buy two food bowls that are dishwasher-safe. I recommend a stainless steel bowl because Einstein will be unable to eat the bowl if he is still hungry after his meal. If Einstein is going to stay in an exercise pen or crate all day, buy a two-quart stainless bucket and a double-headed bolt snap. Clip the bucket to the inside of the crate or ex-pen. If you leave water in a bowl, there is a good chance that Einstein might tip the bowl over and be left without the means of getting a drink. Make sure the water bowl you use in the house is heavy so that Einstein is unable to roll it around in a game of canine soccer.

SOMETHING TO CHEW ON

Young puppies chew on anything they can get their teeth on. For some reason, they always seem to prefer the leg of the table to the toy you have just spent your hard-earned dollars to purchase. The inexpensive chew toy I recommend is something you can make yourself and should appeal to Einstein more than any table leg. What is it? A natural soup bone! Before you bring Einstein home, go to your grocery store and buy several packages of soup bones. Unless your puppy is on the large size, if the bones are more than three inches long, ask the butcher if he can cut them in half. At home, remove as much fat and gristle from the bones as possible. Place the bones on a broiling rack in an oven set at 350°. Bake them for about forty-five minutes. Then take them out of the oven and allow them to cool. Put the bones in the freezer and use as needed. To recycle the bone, stuff the center with peanut butter or something tasty the dog likes to eat.

SHAMPOO

When Einstein is a puppy, you will probably want to give him a bath occasionally. Visit a pet store or your veterinarian and buy shampoo recommended by the sales associate. If you are concerned about Einstein getting fleas, consult with your veterinarian regarding what products to use for these pests. Some flea shampoos are extremely toxic to dogs, and you should only purchase flea shampoo from someone knowledgeable about its use. A grocery store is not the place to purchase dog shampoo! If fleas and ticks are a problem in your area, there are special products you can apply to your dog's skin that kill ticks and inhibit the reproduction of the flea. Again, consult your veterinarian about the use of these products.

BRUSH AND/OR COMB

If Einstein is purebred, his breeder or a book about his breed can recommend the type of grooming tools necessary to keep his coat in top shape. If you are uncertain what type of brush or comb would be best, take Einstein to a pet supply shop that offers a grooming service. The sales associate can confer with the groomer as to what grooming tools would best suit your needs. There are so many different combs and brushes on the market that the choices can be overwhelming.

A LEASH

If you do not purchase a retractable leash, you will need to buy a regular leash so you can take Einstein safely out for a walk. A six-foot leash is best. Most dog owners are drawn to the colorful nylon leashes that are on the market today. However, these leashes have a couple of disadvantages. A nylon leash can slip through your hands and give you rope burn when Einstein takes off in hot pursuit of the neighbor's cat. Nylon leashes do not have "give," and Einstein can get quite a jolt when he reaches the end of it. Leather leashes, although dull by comparison, will not slip through your hands, and in addition, they have "give." Remember that Einstein will be able to chew both types of leashes quite easily. However, do not consider buying a chain leash. These are hard on your hands and can also injure your dog should they get wrapped around his leg, as leashes sometimes do.

A CHECK CORD

This is something you make yourself, and you will use it both indoors and outside. A check cord is like an extension of your arm. It allows you to catch Einstein when he is at a distance from you. I recommend a check cord of six to eight feet in length to wear in the house and another of fifteen to twenty feet for Einstein to wear outdoors. The thickness of the check cord is based on Einstein's size. If he is small, a piece of drapery cord will make an appropriate check cord. For larger dogs, you can use something heavier like clothesline. I make my check cords out of a nylon rope called twist cord. You can find it at most hardware or home improvement stores. It is light in weight but fairly thick and easy to grab hold of. Burn both ends with a match so the cord does not fray. Then fasten a dog-leash-type snap to one end. You might wonder why you would use a check cord instead of a leash. Check cords are usually lighter in weight, so it is less noticeable to the dog when he is wearing one. Check cords can also be made longer than most leashes, so you do not have to get as close to Einstein to catch him. Finally, check cords are considerably cheaper to purchase than a leash, and there is a good possibility that your puppy might chew through whatever is attached to his collar. Your puppy will only wear a check cord when you are there to supervise him. This way, you can prevent the cord from becoming entangled around a piece of furniture or a tree.

NONESSENTIAL ITEMS FOR EINSTEIN

SQUEAKY TOYS, SOFT TOYS, BALLS, TUG TOYS

Puppy teeth are very sharp and can easily destroy a multitude of toys. The only item that should go into Einstein's stomach is food. When you buy any commercial toy, be sure it is large enough that Einstein cannot swallow it. Soft toys are not recommended. Einstein can easily ingest the cloth or stuffing, and you may end up with an expensive visit to the vet. Puppies can easily remove the squeakers from most toys, and they also can be easily swallowed. If you give Einstein a soft or squeaky toy then you should limit his play to the time when you and he can interact. When the game is over, remove them. A hard rubber ball with a bell inside is a good choice for a toy, particularly if you have a puppy that likes to retrieve. If you decide that you must play tug-of-war with your puppy, be sure the tug toy is of sufficient length that your hands stay well away from Einstein's teeth when he grabs the other end. Puppies do not mean to bite, but in the excitement of the game this sometimes happens if your hands are too close to his mouth. Nylabones are safe toys on which a puppy can chew. Rawhide chews are reasonably safe but can cause an intestinal blockage if swallowed in large chunks. If you are concerned about what items might not be good for Einstein to chew on, talk to your veterinarian about what he considers safe for a puppy.

Many puppy owners feel the need to shower their puppies with toys. They believe the more toys the puppy has to play with, the less trouble he will get into. This certainly is not the case. If you give your puppy only two or three toys, he will quickly learn which toys are his and that all the other things in the house belong to you!

Dog Bed, Pillow, or Pad

These items are like soft toys, easy to destroy and swallow. A puppy does not need anything soft on which to lie. Whatever you give him to lie on, he may eat or soil. If you put a piece of carpet in the bottom of his crate, you will only teach Einstein that it is acceptable to eat carpet. Later, when he relaxes in the living room and eats a hole in the rug, who is at fault?

Baby Gates

If you live in an open-plan house where there is no means of confining Einstein, you should invest in an ex-pen or baby gate. You should prevent a young puppy from having the run of the house. An exercise pen is a wiser choice because a puppy can only chew what you leave in the pen with him. If you "gate" Einstein in the kitchen, you may quickly discover he has a taste for kitchen cabinets and chairs! Additionally, many puppies learn how to climb over baby gates or knock them down. This can be disastrous if it happens while you are away from the house. However, if you spend a lot of time at home you will find extra-long baby gates for dogs are available in many dog supply catalogs. These are made specifically for those extra-large openings found in open-plan houses today.

Nail Clippers

A dog should have his nails clipped on a regular basis, at least once a month. This is not an easy task for an inexperienced dog owner. Many people elect to take their dogs to a grooming shop or to the veterinarian to have this service performed. Should you decide to cut Einstein's nails yourself, then ask for suggestions for the correct style of nail clipper at the local pet supply house.

CHAPTER 8

Puppy Proofing Your Home

There are a number of dangers lurking in your home, waiting for Einstein's arrival. When there is a toddler in the house, parents move breakable objects out of reach of tiny hands. They make sure cabinet doors cannot be opened and plug electrical outlets. You will need to take similar precautions before you come home with Einstein.

Chair and table legs fit nicely in a puppy's mouth, and couch cushions shred as easily as fuzzy toys. More than twenty years ago, one of my students learned a bitter lesson on how easily a puppy can destroy couch cushions. The previous week in puppy class I had given my sermon on chewing and related problems. As usual, I had

◀ Puppies love to chew on shrubs and excavate the grounds. *Photo by Margret Taylor. Mixed-breed.*

recommended the use of a crate to prevent a puppy from chewing while the owner was gone. This particular student preferred to use a baby gate to confine his puppy. That Sunday afternoon, I got a telephone call from this student. This grown man was actually in tears. Apparently, he and his wife had spent two years saving for a couch for their home. The couch had cost $1,000, a lot of money in those days. They had it delivered the day before. On Sunday morning, my student and his wife had attended church while their puppy remained home alone, left in the kitchen behind the baby gate. Beau managed to knock the gate over, and as he explored, he encountered the large stuffed cushions of the new couch. When my student arrived home, he discovered what his puppy had been up to while he had been listening to a sermon different from the one I had given earlier in the week. It was too bad he had not listened better in class. There was a happy conclusion, however. They did not take Beau to the shelter but bought a crate instead. One more case of closing the kennel door after the dog got out!

Chewed furniture and couch cushions are not potentially lethal unless the puppy ingests some of the stuffing. These items just cost money to replace. On the other hand, electric cords plugged into a wall socket are easy to chew on and can severely burn a puppy's mouth if he does so. In fact, many puppies are electrocuted each year when they chew on these items.

You should remove any small object that a puppy might swallow from the area where Einstein will be living. Certain houseplants are poisonous to dogs. Toilet deodorizer that stops the toilet bowl from staining can be harmful. Dogs do not discriminate between toilet bowls and water bowls when they want to get a drink of water, and humans often forget to close the lid on the toilet.

When a puppy is in residence, keep all closet and cabinet doors closed. Shoes are particularly attractive to puppies, possibly because they smell so strongly of you! If you have a trash container in the kitchen, make sure the lid is firmly secured. If that is not possible, place the trash can inside one of the kitchen cabinets or in the pantry. A puppy can easily upset a trash can and will find the contents delectable. The following story is true and brings to light just how easily fatal accidents can happen, right in the house. A friend of mine had to go on a business trip. Rather than board her dog in a kennel she preferred to have someone stay at her house to look after her dog. Her dog was a chowhound who would eat anything in the way of food. My friend cautioned the house sitter not to leave any food accessible to the dog. One day, the sitter consumed a large bag of corn chips before leaving the house but did not take the time to place the bag in the trash can, which was secured in the pantry. The corn chip bag was empty when my friend's dog stuck her head into it to get to the remaining crumbs. When the sitter returned a few hours later, the dog had suffocated. Many items that you store under the sink can be toxic to dogs, so be sure your puppy cannot open the lower cabinet doors.

Your garage can also be a dangerous place for your puppy. You may not notice when your car's radiator overflows onto the floor. Antifreeze attracts dogs with its sweet taste, but it is deadly if ingested. About the time Beau destroyed the couch, I had another student training with me who could not afford to purchase a crate. She came home from school one day to discover her dog had become ill in the bedroom and had soiled the floor. She left her dog in the garage while she cleaned up the mess. She did not realize that her car had leaked antifreeze on the floor of the garage. A few minutes later, when she went into the garage to release the dog, the dog was having some sort of seizure. She rushed the dog to the vet, but it died from antifreeze poisoning.

A puppy can easily swallow nuts and bolts. You would be amazed at the different items a veterinarian has removed from a dog's stomach or intestines. Recently, one of my veterinary friends who specializes in surgery removed both a Mark McGwire and a Sammy Sosa baseball from the stomach of a shepherd. The dog's owner was a baseball scout! This was a very expensive operation, in more ways than one!

A favorite snack for a puppy is rocks. It is hard to imagine that puppies would enjoy chewing on rocks, much less swallowing them, but they do it all the time. Most of the time, smaller rocks pass through the puppy's system quite easily, while on other occasions you will have to have one surgically removed. If you leave a puppy out in the yard all day while you are gone, he may amuse himself by chewing on rocks. If he is digging to China then do not leave him out in the yard unattended, particularly if you have an in-ground sprinkler system. I know of someone who had to replace the entire sprinkler system because the dog bit off every sprinkler as it came up out of the ground to water the grass.

Puppies love to chew on shrubs and excavate the grounds. While eating shrubs may not be harmful to a puppy, it is certainly harmful to your landscaping. However, some shrubs are poisonous to dogs. If Einstein decides to change the look of your landscaping, place a temporary fence around the shrubs to protect them. You may wish to consider contacting your local nursery or county extension office to find out which shrubs and houseplants are poisonous to dogs.

Finally, if you have a fenced yard, check the fence line to make sure there are no low spots where Einstein can squeeze under the fence. Furthermore, check for holes in the fence and put a lock on the gate. You may not be the only person in the neighborhood to think Einstein is cute. Dognapping is a lucrative business. Even if nobody wants to steal your dog, meter readers may leave an unlocked gate open by accident. If you have a swimming pool, make certain Einstein cannot gain access to the pool area. Like children, many dogs drown each year by falling into the pool when there is nobody around to see the mishap.

A product of today's age of technology is the underground fence system. This type of fence works through the use of a radio signal. Your dog wears a collar that contains a receiver. When your dog, wearing his receiver, gets within a certain distance of the cable buried around the property line, the collar beeps a warning. If your dog ignores the warning and continues to get closer to the cable, the collar then gives him an electrical stimulation.

Most dogs can be trained to respect the fence. However, you do have to train them. They will not understand about boundaries if you simply put the collar on them and then turn them loose. They must understand that if the collar beeps, they must turn back toward the house, rather than continue on their merry way. They will soon learn that if they proceed any further they will get zapped. It takes a week or more to train your dog to know where the boundaries lie, and it requires that you spend about fifteen minutes a day out in the yard with him to introduce him to the location of "the fence." In addition, a puppy under four months of age is simply too young to be trained for this type of fence.

A few dogs have been known to grit their teeth and leave the yard anyway, even when properly introduced to the fence. If the power goes out in the house, the fence becomes inactive. Many dogs, once trained, never go near the property line again. Others, however, constantly test the fence's security and will leave the property immediately if their collars do not beep. Occasionally, a dog gets out by accident, and then he will get zapped by the collar when trying to return home.

One day a friend of mine forgot to put the receiver collars on her two Dobermans. She lived on six acres, and the underground fence encompassed the entire property. Without her knowledge, two deer were browsing on her land, and the dogs came upon them as they were running around. They did what comes naturally to most dogs—they chased the deer. As deer and dogs went racing across her property, my friend suddenly realized that neither dog was wearing the receiver collar. She was in a panic wondering where her dogs might end up. However, when the Dobermans reached the perimeter of the property where their collars usually buzzed, they both screeched to a stop and watched the deer run off through the brush.

For people who live in a location where fencing is not permitted, this type of fence is a godsend. If you live on acreage and cannot afford a standard fence but wish to give your dog the run of your property, then this type of fence may be the answer. These fences can cover as much as twenty acres, depending on the type of transmitter you purchase. However, they do have their drawbacks.

What people fail to remember is that even though a dog has been trained not to leave its yard, there is nothing to prevent another dog or some other animal from coming onto the property. You must have a safe area for your dog to enter in case he is attacked. Out in the West, javelina pigs are of major concern, and they will attack a dog on sight. These pests roam freely even in suburban areas and are a protected animal except during a short hunting season. Free-roaming dogs are another hazard. They may even follow your dog right into your house if his way of escape is through a doggie door.

If you elect to install an underground fence, then you should never go off and leave your dog outside, unless you can confine him to a kennel run or a regular fenced-in area. Your concern must be for something entering your property, rather than for your dog leaving. However, underground fences malfunction on occasion, so rather than take the chance of the fence not working correctly, confine Einstein whenever you leave. As long as you do, then you will not need to worry about what might be happening at home while you are gone.

CHAPTER 9

Teaching Your Puppy the Right Way to Live

Before you leave to collect Einstein, take a few minutes to consider the following. The question most often asked by puppy owners is "When is the best time to start training my puppy?" The answer is "From the moment he enters your home."

There are three main reasons why an owner finds his dog another home. The first is for house-soiling problems. The second is because of destructive chewing. The third is because the dog bites. You can avoid these issues if you take the time to train your puppy from the moment he enters your life.

◄When is the best time to start training a puppy? From the moment you bring him home. Ramsey's Lacey CDX, HIC, CGC, owned by Ann Ramsey. *Photo by Ann Ramsey. Pembroke Welsh Corgi, Herding Group.*

When a dog that lives in the wild leaves the den to eliminate, it does not matter where he chooses to do his business. Nor does it matter on which objects he chooses to chew. When a dog lives in our society, we have to teach him the appropriate location in which to eliminate and what are appropriate objects on which to chew. When your puppy soils the living room carpet of your house or chews on the corner of the coffee table, he is not being a bad puppy. He has simply soiled in an unacceptable location or chewed on an unacceptable object, that is all. He has yet to learn "the rules" of living in our society. It is your responsibility to teach him the right way to live.

If you ask dog owners what they consider the most important social skill their dogs can learn, 99 percent will say, "To be house-broken." So, before you drive off to collect Einstein, let us look at how to housebreak a puppy. It is not difficult to teach if you follow a few simple guidelines.

SURVIVING HOUSEBREAKING

MAKING USE OF THE "DEN"

Dogs do not like to soil their dens, the area in which they have to sleep. Given the choice, a puppy will leave the den to eliminate somewhere else. Puppies recognize the area in which to eliminate by the smell of urine or feces. In your home, Einstein's crate or ex-pen becomes his den. If you allow him the freedom of the entire house, he will leave his area when he has to eliminate. When he goes into another room to "do his business," he is not being a bad puppy; he is doing something quite natural for a dog. He is keeping his den clean by soiling some other place. Once his scent is in that spot, he will return there any chance he gets.

A puppy between the ages of seven and twelve weeks will have limited bladder and bowel control. I have discovered that many new puppy owners are much better trainers than I am. They inform me that their puppies are housebroken by the time they are eight weeks old. I must be doing something wrong because I do not expect my puppies to be housebroken until they are somewhere between six and nine months of age! In fact, when a dog owner tells me her puppy is housebroken, what she really means to say is that she gets the puppy out in time, and this is the secret of house-training. No puppy has the same kind of muscle control to control elimination like that of an older dog. Between the ages of three and four months, you can expect a puppy that is wide awake and running about to be able to control his bladder for up to an hour without needing to be taken outside. Between the ages of four and six months, he should not need to be taken out more than every couple of hours. By the time your puppy is six months old, he should be almost totally housebroken. However, puppies sometimes have accidents, just as young children occasionally wet their pants. Puppies and young children get so involved in play that they sometimes forget to get to the bathroom in time.

THE "POTTY" AREA

In the beginning, the moment your puppy wakes up from a nap you will need to take him to the area where you wish him to relieve himself. Always take him to the same spot every time. Remember that the smell of urine will encourage him to eliminate there. Preferably, the spot will be out-of-doors, unless you live in an apartment. If that is where you reside and you have a balcony, you may want to give him an elimination area out there. (See Chapter 11, "Latchkey Pups.") No matter where you live, you will need to take Einstein to his spot immediately after he has eaten and after he has had a drink. When you reach that spot, and he begins circling and sniffing, keep repeating a cue word that means, "Go potty." Any word will do, as long as you and all family members are consistent with its use. Your puppy will eventually associate the word with the action of eliminating, a real time-saver if you are ever in a hurry or when traveling and you need him to eliminate in a strange place.

Any time you take your puppy to his spot, you should stay there with him so you can let him know, by praising him, that he is eliminating in an acceptable place. Why is it so important to stay with him? First, if you scold him for eliminating in an inappropriate place inside your house and then praise him for doing his business in the correct location, he will start to make the connection between right and wrong. Second, if you stay there with him you will not be bringing him back into the house before he has finished doing his business. Most puppies have a schedule of elimination, and if they have not completed the process and you let them back into the house, they are likely to continue on your living room carpet. This is particularly so first thing in the morning. A puppy confined during the night is going to be happy to see you and may not want to take the time to do all his business. If, under normal circumstances, he piddles twice before he defecates, and you leave him outside while you fix a pot of coffee, you will not know if he became sidetracked and only piddled once or never defecated at all. When you let him back inside and reach into the fridge for the milk, he may go off and piddle on the dining room carpet because he had not finished eliminating outside. It takes more than five minutes to clean up a mess on the carpet, so get up five minutes earlier, and remain outside with Einstein. There is a third reason to stay outside with Einstein. If his stool is loose, he might be coming down with a virus. You may want to call your veterinarian before you feed him his next meal or make arrangements for someone to come in and let him out several times during the day. Let's say he does not defecate for several trips outside. This might indicate that he has swallowed something and has an intestinal blockage. No matter how careful you try to be, a puppy can ingest an object that you would think would be impossible to swallow. This happened once to one of my friends. She had a fenced yard and did not go out with her puppy when she put him outside to eliminate. She also had an older dog, and both animals ate in the same room. She had no idea that the puppy had a blockage because his food always disappeared. Obviously, the older dog was getting double rations. Finally, the puppy started acting strangely, and she took him to the vet. The puppy had swallowed a huge rock, and unfortunately, the intestines had suffered such trauma that there was nothing to be done. Your puppy's stool is a good indication of his health. The only way you know if there is a problem is to be there to watch him eliminate.

The "Match Trick"

Occasionally, Einstein may not defecate when you take him out-side, but you know he needs to go. You also know that if you bring him back inside and then leave for work or go to bed, he will need to go out within a short time. Is there anything you can you do to avert this situation? For years, professional dog handlers have had a trick in their pockets that a pet owner can use to full advantage. They call it the "match trick." Keep on hand a book of paper matches, the kind often given out in restaurants. If Einstein refus-es to defecate, and you need to leave him in his den for several hours, break off a match from the book. Please do not consider striking it. Instead, wet the end that you would normally light. You can put some saliva on it or run it under water from the faucet. Take hold of Einstein by the collar and lift up his tail with your other hand. Let go of the collar and with that hand insert the strik-ing end of the match into his rectum. Leave enough of the match protruding so that you can remove it if necessary. Within a few sec-onds most dogs will start to circle and then defecate. During this time, you should be offering your verbal cue to "Go potty." The sulfur of the match tip irritates the rectum, which in turn stimulates him to defecate. Occasionally, this trick does not work, so after a minute or so if Einstein has not defecated, perhaps he has no need to go. Remove the match by grasping the end that is protruding from the anus. If you are concerned that using a match is harmful, you can always purchase infant suppositories to use instead. The match trick is a good way to condition a puppy to defecate on com-mand, if you are having problems getting him to eliminate when you take him outside.

Planning and Scheduling

In order to make housebreaking even easier, you should keep Einstein on the same schedule, day in and day out. You should feed him his meals at the same time every day. You should get up at the same time every morning, even on the weekend, until Einstein is fully housebroken. You should go to bed at the same time every night, the later the better. The earlier you feed Einstein his evening meal, the sooner the food will pass through his system. This way, there will be less chance of him needing to go out in the middle of the night. When you give your puppy definite mealtimes, you will know when he needs to go out because you will know when he last ate. If you place your puppy on a self-feeding program, you will never know when your puppy might have eaten some of his food, and therefore you can only guess when to let him outside.

Do not let Einstein drink water all evening long. Remove his water bowl and close the lids on the toilets. You can give him a drink several times during the evening if the weather is hot or if he has been running around. You want him to go to bed with a relatively empty bladder. About thirty minutes before you put Einstein to bed for the night, give him one last drink. Some puppies drink just for the sake of drinking, so only put a couple of inches of water in the bottom of the bowl.

PICK UP THE PAPERS

What about allowing your puppy to eliminate on newspapers placed somewhere in the house? The reason you take him outside is so that Einstein never thinks that eliminating in the house is acceptable. If, for example, you acquire a puppy in the middle of winter and you feel it is too cold to take him outside, turn part of the garage into a "duty" area, rather than having him use your laundry room. (See Chapter 11.) The rooms in your house all have a similar odors and temperatures, whereas the garage will smell different to your puppy. Because the garage will be cooler in temperature, it will not appear to be part of the house. You want Einstein to understand he must leave the house to do his business, so do not leave papers on the floor and encourage him to use them. However, you may need to leave papers in the ex-pen or crate initially so that if he has an accident while confined it will be relatively easy to clean up. The disadvantage of placing newspapers in his den is that they are easy for him to shred and time consuming for you to pick up.

When Accidents Happen

Finally, accidents are bound to happen. Sometimes it is your fault, and sometimes it is the fault of the puppy. No matter whose fault it is, do not rub his face in his business if he makes a mistake. It will teach him only one thing, and that is to fear you! What do you do if you catch him in the act? In a sharp voice say, "No," "Wrong," or "Hey, what are you doing?" This is a verbal correction, and you use it to stop him from doing the wrong thing. If he is little, pick him up and take him outside. If he is larger, grab him by the collar and rush him to the door. If he restarts eliminating when he reaches his spot, praise him. However, there is a good chance that he will no longer have the urge to go. Your correction may have put him off. If he does not eliminate in his spot, bring him back inside and then confine him so that you can clean up the mess. Before Einstein has his first accident, prepare a spray bottle filled with a mixture of 25 percent white vinegar and 75 percent water. When Einstein has an accident, you want to deter him from returning to that area. Dogs dislike the smell of vinegar and will avoid a spot that smells of vinegar in the future. If he has urinated, first blot up the urine with several layers of paper towel, and then spray the area with the vinegar solution. Blot up the vinegar. If he makes a pile, pick it up with paper towel and flush it down the toilet. However, place the paper towel in the trash, otherwise you might stop up the toilet, creating another mess. Clean the area with carpet cleaner if necessary, and then spray with the vinegar solution. When you let Einstein out of his place of confinement, take him out to relieve himself. He will probably need to go again by then.

What happens if you discover a place in the house that Einstein soiled when you were not watching him? Shame on you! It is your fault. You have not been paying close enough attention to Einstein. Clean it up. It will do no good at all to reprimand your puppy hours or even days later. He will not remember what he has done. Once you have cleaned up the mess, do not forget to spray the area with the vinegar solution. You want to deter Einstein from returning to that same spot in the future.

No matter how careful some owners are when it comes to teaching their puppy the acceptable place to eliminate, they may still end up with a problem dog. Dogs that soil the house are not being vindictive. They just do not understand that eliminating inside is unacceptable. This often occurs when an owner has been so diligent in house-training that the puppy never had an accident inside when he was younger. For this reason, the dog never learned that eliminating inside was wrong. Sometimes a dog has to be wrong in order to understand when he is right.

Years ago this happened to me with one of my dogs. Even at almost a year of age, my dachshund would occasionally soil the house. I would never see her do it, so I never got a chance to reprimand her. How would I be sure to catch her in the act? The technique I used with her I have since used successfully with clients' dogs that have had similar problems. You need to choose a day when you have the time to wait for the dog to make a mistake. For many people, this would be on a weekend. When you get up in the morning, do not let your dog out no matter how many times he runs to the door. Instead, sit down with the newspaper and a cup of coffee or tea. Pretend to read the paper, but instead keep an eye on your dog. If your dog starts to sneak away, do not say a word. Lay down the paper and quietly follow the dog, preferably in your bare feet so you do not make any sound. If nothing happens, return to pretending to read the paper while still watching the dog. Sometimes the wait is not long, and sometimes it can be several hours. Eventually your dog is going to eliminate in the house, and you will be able to catch him in the act. You are going to create a scene and, hopefully, a big impression on Einstein. Often it only takes one correction to fix the problem. However, you should set up the same scenario for the following day or weekend. If your dog keeps going to the door the second time you try to set him up, then you probably should let him outside. Give him a few days, to see if your correction worked. If he has any more accidents, you are going to have to repeat this procedure.

HOME SWEET HOME

Before you bring Einstein home with you, make sure you have followed the guidelines in Chapter 8, "Puppy Proofing Your Home." Moreover, decide ahead of time in which area you will train Einstein to eliminate. When you leave the breeder's house or the animal shelter, ask if you can take some soiled newspaper with you so you can place it on the ground when you reach your destination. Remember that dogs are attracted to the smell of urine, and you want your puppy to be attracted to the area where you want him to eliminate. When you get out of the car, the first thing you should do is to take Einstein to the designated area where you want him to relieve himself. Put the soiled newspapers on the ground and encourage him to sniff them. You may have to wait several minutes before Einstein squats to piddle. When he does, praise him and then bring him indoors.

When you bring Einstein into the house, take him directly to the area that you will use for his den. If you followed the suggestions in Chapters 7 and 8, you will have purchased an ex-pen or baby gates so that you can prevent Einstein from having the run of the house. Do not invite the entire neighborhood in to meet the new addition. Your puppy will be stressed from leaving the only home he has known, so give him a chance to settle in before you have "open house" for Einstein.

If you have a home-cooked bone (see Chapter 7), give it to Einstein. With luck he will lie down and start to chew on it, and you will be able to relax. If Einstein becomes restless, take him out to the duty area and follow the guidelines on housebreaking. If he decides to take a nap, put him in his crate. There is a good reason for doing this. Unless you confine him to his crate, when he wakes up, the first thing he will do is stretch and then leave the area to eliminate. Unless you happen to notice he has awakened, it is unlikely that you will get him out in time. However, if you put him in his crate, when he awakes he will start to fuss because he wishes to be let out. When you hear him whining you can open the door and carry him outside. Why carry him? If you allow him to walk to the door, he may stop to squat on the way! So, carry him until he is a little older, when he has become accustomed to the routine and knows where to go when you let him out of the crate.

SURVIVING DESTRUCTIVE CHEWING

PREVENTION RATHER THAN CURE

Little kids like to handle objects; the more breakable the better, it seems. Children learn about life partly through touch. Puppies learn about life through taste and smell. Puppies investigate their world with their noses and then put things in their mouths. Quite often, they select a chair leg, couch cushion, or your favorite pair of shoes. When you have a puppy in the house, remember that prevention is better than cure. Do not leave your puppy in a place where he will find something on which to chew unless it is one of his toys. Any time you cannot supervise Einstein, you should confine him to his crate or ex-pen. You should do this when you are taking a shower or balancing the checkbook. A baby gate can confine him to a certain area of your house, but it cannot prevent him from chewing something in the room. If you confine him to an exercise pen or a crate, he can only chew on whatever you place in there with him.

SWEET DREAMS

In the beginning, a puppy often cries when you leave him alone. You have to remember that, until now, your puppy has been able to snuggle up with his mother and littermates. Suddenly, he discovers he is all by himself. He will adjust in a few days. Unfortunately, when their puppies start to cry some owners believe it is because the puppies hate the crate or ex-pen and immediately give up using it. It should come as no surprise that these are the puppies that often grow up to be dogs with destructive chewing and house-soiling problems.

You may not get much sleep the first few nights Einstein takes up residence. He will be lonely and will call out to his mother to come and find him. Some owners are opposed to allowing their dogs to sleep in the bedroom, while others would not consider the dog sleeping anywhere else. No matter what your preference, it is advisable to have Einstein sleep in the bedroom in his crate or ex-pen for the first few nights. You can always move him back to his daytime den area once he has become adjusted to his new home. Place his crate or pen right next to the bed if there is room. When you get into bed, put your fingers through the bars of the cage or ex-pen so he can feel your touch. If you have prevented him from sleeping all evening, he will soon be ready to fall asleep. Do not wake him up in the middle of the night to take him outside unless he wakes up and starts to fuss. The advantage of having him in the room with you is that you can let him out when he needs to go, before he has a chance to soil his den. Many seven-week-old puppies can sleep through the night, providing you feed them early, do not let them drink a full bowl of water, and give them plenty of exercise in the hours before bedtime. Remember that a good dog is a tired dog. If you play with Einstein during the evening, when the time comes to go to bed he should be ready to fall asleep. Do not let him settle down for a nap right before it is time for bed.

THE MIDNIGHT SERENADE

At first, if he cries at night, it is only fair to comfort him. However, once you feel that he has adjusted to being an "only puppy," you will have to deal with the midnight serenade should it occur. This is another reason to have Einstein sleep in the bedroom for the first few weeks, if not permanently. There is nothing more frustrating than lying in bed, listening to a puppy barking his head off somewhere else in the house. You know that you are eventually going to have to get up to quiet him, so you might as well keep him in the room with you and remain in bed. My solution to midnight barking is to place a pie pan on top of the crate. If my puppy barks, I tell him, "No, quiet," which is a verbal correction, and if the noise continues, I reach for the pie pan and bang it on the top of the crate. The noise and vibration that it makes is usually enough to quiet the puppy. When he is silent, I tell him he is good and go back to sleep. This, without even having to leave my bed.

For the next few weeks, if you confine Einstein behind a baby gate, plan on spending the evening with him, rather than leaving him confined by himself. When you have a young puppy in the house, you must be willing to make some sacrifices. One of them will be to sit in the kitchen in a straight-backed chair, rather than in your recliner in the living room while you watch your favorite programs on TV. It would be most unwise to take Einstein into the living room with you. If you fall asleep in your recliner, it would be easy for him to wet the floor or even chew a hole in the carpet. I can tell you from my own experience that this can happen.

For the next few months keep all doors to the bedrooms and bathrooms closed so that if Einstein should get away from his den area he cannot get far. These rooms often have clothing, shoes, and children's toys scattered on the floor, things that will be highly tempting for a puppy to chew on.

If you catch Einstein chewing on an inappropriate object, tell him, "No," or "Wrong" in a sharp tone of voice then remove the object from his mouth. Immediately replace the object with something you allow him to have, like a bone or squeaky toy. Once he begins chewing on his toy, praise him. This is the same principle you use when teaching him the acceptable and unacceptable areas for elimination. In addition, if at any other time you notice Einstein chewing on one of his toys, praise him.

Unfortunately, the chewing stage often lasts until a dog is somewhere between eighteen months and two years of age. As your puppy reaches six months of age, he is less likely to chew inappropriately in front of you because you can remind him of "the rules" with a verbal reprimand when you are right there with him. Therefore, you can begin to allow Einstein some freedom in the house, under your supervision. However, whenever you cannot monitor him you should continue to restrict him to his den so that he does not get into trouble.

SURVIVING THOSE PUPPY TEETH

Puppies have very sharp teeth. When your puppy was growing up in the litter, if he bit his mother she would immediately correct him by grabbing hold of him and pinning him to the ground. He would soon learn not to bite down hard. If he bit too hard on a littermate, the other puppy would retaliate or leave him to play with another puppy. When a dog gently puts his teeth on you, he has learned a very important skill called "inhibited" biting. However, you still need to teach him that any biting is not acceptable.

NIP BITING IN THE BUD

Some puppies chew on their owners more than do others. Biting is often directed at people's hands. This is because their hands stroke the puppy and are close to his face. Hands also feed the puppy treats and are close to the puppy's mouth. Some owners foolishly put on heavy gloves so they do not feel the pain of those needle-sharp teeth on their skin. That is the worst thing you can do. You are not addressing the problem. Owners are often at fault because they encourage their puppies to bite by playing roughly with them.

What do you do if Einstein starts to bite on your hands? If it hurts, and it probably will, let him know. Say, "Ouch, ohhh," loudly or make a similar sound. Then walk away from him. This is how his littermates would treat him. There is a good chance that this will not have much impact on Einstein. If he is biting because he is overexcited, then give him a time-out by placing him in his crate or ex-pen. If he continues to bite, is there another alternative? As soon as he begins to bite on your hands, hold onto his lower jaw by placing your thumb across his tongue and your fingers under his chin. This is rather like putting a bit in a horse's mouth. Pull his lower jaw downward, away from his upper jaw, and squeeze. At the same time, tell him sharply, "No biting, no biting." He cannot bite down on your hand when you do this because his upper jaw is fixed. It is only his lower jaw that is hinged. After a few seconds, release the pressure on his jaw. If he stops biting you, praise him. If he bites you again, take hold of his lower jaw, and this time squeeze it harder and hold it for a longer time. You want your puppy to think that when he opens his mouth to bite you his jaw becomes trapped.

When puppies start to teethe, at around four months of age, mouthing problems are likely to increase. Make sure you have plenty of those marrowbones available for Einstein to chew. If you deter a puppy from mouthing early on, biting as an adult is less likely to be a problem. You must nip biting in the bud the first time it happens.

In addition to biting on the owner's hands, many puppies grab hold of clothing and play tug-of-war with your pant legs. This happens more frequently to children. Little children and puppies are not a good combination. They should each have their individual playtime. If you have a puppy and a child, or children, then you must supervise their interaction until the puppy is older. When children are running around the house or yard and squealing with delight, the noise and movement trigger the long-dormant prey drive in most puppies. It is only natural for Einstein to want to chase and catch the prey, which in this instance happens to be your child. You should allow the puppy to interact with the children when they are sitting quietly watching TV, rather than when they are running around the house. You need to come up with a deterrent for biting that an older child might be able to use. If your puppy starts biting on your child's clothing or hands, then have your child squirt him in the face with the vinegar solution. This technique will usually make a puppy turn tail and leave. It does not hurt the puppy physically, nor does it require perfect aim. Dogs dislike the smell of vinegar and having water misted in their faces. They will associate this correction with what they were just doing—biting on your child's clothing or hands.

THE DANGERS OF TUG-OF-WAR

Most owners and their family members delight in playing a game of tug-of-war with their puppies, and most puppies reciprocate with pleasure. Although this game can be a lot of fun, the participants are unwittingly teaching their puppies to growl at them and, in addition, refuse to give up something that the puppies have in their mouths. This is a particularly risky thing to do with a dominant puppy or with a breed disposed to biting. If your puppy is dominant, you should never play any game that will cause him to dominate you until your role of leader is assured. Nor should you ever encourage growling and gripping of objects with a breed known to be aggressive.

If you feel you simply must play tug-of-war with Einstein, then play the game as follows. When Einstein is growling and pulling on the tug toy, tell him, "Let go" and instantly mist him in the face with plain water or, if you believe you need to, the vinegar solution. The moment he lets go of the tug toy, praise him and then give him a treat. You want him to instantly give up the tug toy on command. After a few repetitions, when you tell him, "Let go," do not mist him and see if he lets go without the need for you to do anything negative. If he lets go, praise him and then give him a treat. If he continues to hang on to the toy, repeat the command and then mist him in the face.

In addition to teaching him the command "let go," also teach Einstein the command "leave it" (Chapter 13). If you have a dog that is dominant, you may be able to allow him to play tug-of-war when he is older, after he has had some training. First, he must respond to the command "leave it," and second he must obey other obedience commands like "come" and "stay." If you have that much control over a dominant puppy, it is obvious you have established your role as leader, and your puppy can be allowed to play a game like tug-of-war. However, you must always be the one to end up with the toy when the game ends.

SHOWING EINSTEIN WHO'S THE BOSS

If you picked Einstein out of a litter of puppies and followed the advice in the section on choosing a puppy in Chapter 5, you should not have picked a dominant puppy. If you did not pay attention to those recommendations, or if there were no other puppies with which to compare, you may have come to realize that you have an alpha puppy living in your house. Dominant puppies like to run the show and may challenge you for leadership on a regular basis, unless you establish who is the boss right from the start. Dominant dogs are full of confidence, are smart, and quickly learn whom they can push around. Dominance usually starts to become an issue when a puppy reaches around four months of age. If you suspect you own an alpha dog, this is what you need to do to assure your position as leader of the pack.

DEALING WITH DOMINANCE

In a pack situation, be it a wolf pack or a pride of lions, the leader gets the choice of where he beds down. Therefore, never allow a dominant dog to sleep on the bed with you. In fact, he should not even spend the night in your room. If you suspect Einstein would like to take over as leader, leave his crate in the kitchen or laundry room at night once he is no longer crying out of loneliness. Your bedroom must be the domain of the pack leader, which is you and your spouse or partner. In the wild, the pack leaders always eat first. So, if you suspect Einstein wants to be in charge, always have your meal before you feed him his supper, or if you eat late, do not allow him in the room when you are eating. Whenever you go outside with Einstein, make sure you are the one to go through the door first. If he comes over to you to be petted, make him sit, and then praise him for responding to a command rather than giving him petting for free. If you put these ideas into practice at the first sign of trouble, then you should maintain your role of pack leader without a major battle.

TEACHING EINSTEIN OTHER SOCIAL SKILLS

Even if you do not consider Einstein alpha, another problem that sometimes arises is that your puppy may try to bite when you try to take a possession away from him, particularly when it is something he should not have. From the beginning you should insist that Einstein give up to you whatever he has in his mouth. You do this for a variety of reasons, not just to tease him. There may be a time when he has hold of something dangerous, and you need him to give it up without a fuss. To be fair to Einstein, never try to take anything away from him without first telling him that you are going to remove it. When you do, be sure to return the object to him immediately, or give him something else in exchange. Initially, do not try to take away his favorite toy or bone. Choose something that he is more likely to give up willingly. Tell him something like, "Let me have that." Then remove the object from his mouth. Praise him, and give it back, or offer him a treat. You can call this "a trade," and it is a useful trick to know when raising a puppy.

GUARDING POSSESSIONS

If Einstein is willing to give up his toy, try the same approach when he has something he really wants to keep. Some puppies give up whatever they are chewing on, while others guard possessions with their lives. If the latter is the case with Einstein, be prepared to reprimand him physically. If he growls at you or offers to bite, take him by the scruff of his neck and hold him off the ground so that only his rear toes are making contact with the floor. Look him straight in the eye while you say a few choice words. When you hold him in this manner, he will feel insecure. Put him back on all fours and give him a time-out so he can think about what he has done. Repeat this again a little later on, to see if you have a different response. After all, you are the pack leader, and the subordinate members of the pack always allow the leader to take the "prize." Once your puppy allows you to remove his possessions you must make certain that your spouse and children can do the same. You must put Einstein to the test while you are there to supervise, and to intervene if necessary. Einstein must understand that he must release his possessions to every member of the family group. If you do not address this problem, someone may end up being bitten. Remember that you and your children, if you have any, may know that your puppy likes to guard his toys, but visitors to your house may be unaware of this problem, so deal with it while Einstein is still little.

GUARDING FOOD

A puppy that allows you to take away his toys may have a different attitude about allowing you to remove his food bowl. One day, when Einstein is in the middle of eating, say those same words, "Let me have that," and reach for the bowl. Three things are likely to happen. First, if he is a chowhound he will gobble the food as fast as he can. He will allow you to take the bowl; however, he will try to make sure the bowl is empty! Second, he might say, "OK, Boss, you bought the food, so if you want it, it's all yours." Third, he might say, "Stay away. It's mine." In the latter case, you can either correct him as you might do if he growled over a toy, or you can try another technique. The next time you feed Einstein, put down an empty food bowl, but have his meal available in another container. When he walks over to his bowl to see what is in it, place one piece of food in the bowl. Once he has eaten that, place another piece in the bowl and continue in this manner until he has eaten his entire meal. Let him realize that he only gets his food from you and that you are not trying to take the food away. Although you expect Einstein to relinquish a toy to your children, food is a different story. Your children should learn never to bother any dog when it is eating. Even the best natured dogs are sometimes untrustworthy around a food bowl, so children should learn to leave a dog alone when food is involved.

Food guarding can become a serious problem. We once went to the home of a lady who was unable to enter the kitchen while her dog was eating, for fear of being attacked. If one piece of food remained on the floor, her dog would guard it. The dog would keep the owner out of the kitchen for hours at a time. This situation had gone on for several years before she finally decided to address it. The solution we came up with was to feed the dog in the laundry room, with the door closed. Not an ideal situation, but at least the owner could enter her kitchen anytime she wanted.

In addition to housebreaking, chewing, and biting, there are several additional behaviors that you need to address. Are you are going to allow your dog to get on the furniture? What do you do when a puppy steals food off the counters or takes things out of the trash? How do you stop your puppy from jumping on you or on visitors coming to the door? How do you prevent him from barking unnecessarily?

FURNITURE OR FLOOR?

Some dog owners do not mind dog hair all over the couch or the bed. Others would really prefer not to let the dog past the kitchen. Whatever your pleasure, everyone in the family must agree on what the puppy is going to be allowed to do when it comes to getting on the furniture. Owners of smaller dogs are more likely to allow their puppies to get up on the bed or couch than the owners of larger breeds. If you are not going to allow Einstein on the furniture, then do not sit in a chair and hold him in your lap when he is a little puppy. If you do, you are giving him mixed signals. This does not prevent you from holding Einstein in your lap. You will just have to sit on the floor when you do so. If you have children in the house, they often encourage a puppy to get up on the bed with them, and then the parent wonders why the puppy suddenly gets up on the couch. Remember that you are not dealing with a human where you can explain that a bed is not a couch. To a puppy, anything he can climb on he considers furniture. If you do not want your puppy to get on the furniture, you must push him off every time he tries, at the same time telling him, "No, get off." If Einstein continues to get on the furniture, clip a short check cord to his collar. (See Chapter 7, "The Puppy Starter Kit.") When you catch him up on the furniture, grab the end of the check cord, tell him to "Get off," and then use the cord to remove him from the piece of furniture on which he is laying. Praise him once he is back on the floor.

HIGH-TECH TRAINING AIDS

Dog owners today are lucky to be living in the technological age. There are some excellent training aids available on the market today that make dealing with problem behaviors much easier than in the past. If Einstein continues to get on one particular piece of furniture, you may wish to invest in a product called a Scat Mat. The Scat Mat comes in several sizes. It is a thin plastic mat with electrical wires running across it, which give off an unpleasant sensation when a dog steps or lies on the mat. It will not physically harm the dog, but he will not want to remain on the mat for even a moment. In addition, the Scat Mat works effectively when placed in a doorway to keep a dog out of certain rooms of the house or from going upstairs.

Years ago, before the Scat Mat was invented, we did a behavior consultation in the home of a medium-sized breed often known for its nasty disposition. The owners' most pressing problem was that they had been unable to eat at the table for the past year. Sparky had taken the table for his den, and on the table he resided night and day. During this time, his owners had eaten every meal off TV trays while sitting on the couch. We showed them how to forcefully remove Sparky from the table by the use of a check cord. In addition, we helped them with other problem behaviors. On a follow-up telephone call, they told us how happy they were with the outcome of our visit. I expected to hear that Sparky no longer got on the table. I was disappointed to learn that the table was still his den. However, the owner was thrilled because Sparky now got off the table when commanded, so the family was finally able to eat all their meals sitting down at the table. Had the Scat Mat already been invented the outcome would have been different. Sparky would have had to find a new den.

Dogs are smart. They know they are not supposed to get on the furniture, so when they hear you coming, they jump off before you catch them on the couch. The only way you know of their transgression is that the couch cushion is still warm to the touch! There is another training aid available that can help you train Einstein to stay off the furniture. It is aptly called a Tattle Tale. This product is sensitive to vibration, so when your dog gets up on the couch the movement causes the Tattle Tale to emit a shrill sound. Even if your dog ignores the noise, which is unlikely, it will alert you to the fact he is on the couch, and you can rush into the room to correct him.

To Catch a Thief

Food stealing can be frustrating. I have had my dinner stolen by a dog on more than one occasion. One of my students was having a dinner party one night. She had made three dozen sticky buns, and while she was waiting for the yeast to rise she went to the grocery store to buy something she had forgotten to get for the meal. When she returned, her dog had somehow gotten up on the counter and eaten every one of the thirty-six buns. That in itself was bad enough, but she knew the dough had not finished rising and would quickly swell in the warmth of the dog's stomach! She had an expensive visit to the vet's office and no time to make more buns for the dinner party.

Some dogs steal food any chance they get, while others do not care that much about eating. Food stealing is just like destructive chewing in that prevention is better than cure. If you have a dog that tries to steal food from the counter or your dinner plate, you may have to confine him when there is food around. Food stealing is one of the most difficult behaviors to eliminate.

If you have a dog large enough to reach the counter, you can put a Scat Mat on the countertop. Place some delicacy on top of the Scat Mat. When Einstein puts his feet on the counter to see what might be worth stealing, he will feel an unpleasant sensation when he touches the mat. If you do not want to go to the expense of buying a Scat Mat, for only pennies you can booby-trap the counter. Cut a piece of cardboard about six inches wider than the countertop. Then lay the cardboard on top of the counter. Stack ten to twelve empty soda cans, filled with a few pebbles, on the rear of the cardboard. In front of the cans, place something delectable. When Einstein places his feet on the cardboard that is sticking out beyond the countertop, he will dislodge the cardboard and flip the soda cans on top of his head. He will not get hurt, but he will certainly get a surprise! A correction that does not come from you is often very effective.

Sometimes a larger dog puts his feet up on the counter when you are preparing a meal. Warn him to "Get off" as you might if he were trying to get on the furniture. If he persists, give him a good shove sideways, as you repeat the words, "Get off." Occasionally, if your dog is persistent, you will have to make a stronger correction. When he puts his feet on the counter right beside you, rap the top of his feet hard with your hand.

Although I no longer have any dogs that are likely to steal food off the counter or table, I have in years past. Therefore, I have conditioned myself never to leave food out if I have to leave the room and I have a dog in the house. Before leaving the room I place the food up high, somewhere I know a dog cannot reach, like the top of the refrigerator. Otherwise, I put it in the oven, microwave, or fridge. Sometimes it is easier to train the owner rather than the dog!

Another annoying habit is stealing trash. Dogs appear to have a penchant for Kleenex® and, even worse, sanitary napkins. Puppies are usually worse than older dogs when it comes to stealing from the trash. Again, prevention is better then cure. You can often put the bathroom trash container inside the vanity, if there is one, or keep the bathroom door closed. You can place the kitchen trash container under the sink or in the pantry. If you cannot or will not make any concessions in this area, then a Tattle Tale works well to alert you when Einstein puts his head into the trash container. Place a trash bin somewhere you know Einstein will go, and in it place some wadded up newspaper with Kleenex® and the Tattle Tale at the top. When the Tattle Tale alerts you that Einstein is in the trash, you can go rushing into the room to confront him. You can also booby-trap a trash container in a similar manner to that of the kitchen counter. Tie a piece of cord around several pieces of Kleenex® and place them on top of the trash. Next, attach the cord to a piece of cardboard, which you have placed on the kitchen counter or the tank of the toilet. On top of the cardboard, place your empty soda cans. When Einstein grabs the Kleenex® and makes a run for it, the soda cans will come raining down on him.

A puppy often gets great enjoyment out of having you chase after him while he is racing around with Kleenex® in his mouth. Shredded Kleenex® makes a real mess on the carpet. If you are having a problem in this area, one way to solve it is for Einstein to wear his check cord. When he goes diving under the bed with his spoils, you will no longer have to crawl under there to get him. All you have to do is pull on the end of the cord that is trailing behind him and drag him out from under the bed. This game will lose its appeal once he discovers you can catch him easily and remove his prize.

THAT OVERPOWERING GREETING

Jumping up on people is another annoying habit. Many dog owners allow their dogs to jump on them and then wonder why the dog jumps on the guests. Why do dogs jump up in the first place? When dogs greet each other when out for a walk in the park or on a trail in the wild, they sniff each other on the muzzle. When your dog jumps up to greet you, he is only trying to sniff your muzzle, or the muzzle of your visitors. The problem is that your muzzle, and those of your guests, happens to be several feet above his own! If you and your friends would come through the door on all fours, he would not have to jump up on you in order to say hello. However, this means of entering the house not practical.

When Einstein is very young, discourage him from jumping on you when you greet him by getting down on his level instead. As he gets a little older, teach him to sit on command. (See Chapter 13.) When you come in the door and he starts jumping up on you, have him sit before you make a fuss over him. Some dogs are so delighted to see you, or anyone else for that matter, that having them sit rarely works. In that case, they are going to have to learn to keep their feet on the ground while they are cavorting about the room in a high level of excitement. The trusty vinegar spray works well in this instance. When you enter the room hold the spray bottle of the vinegar solution behind your back. When Einstein starts to jump up on you, produce the bottle and spray him in the face with the vinegar solution. As you do so, tell him to "Get off." With this treatment, most dogs will put some distance between you and them. Call him to you, and then have him sit. Praise him for sitting. Then tell him how happy you are to see him. If he is a large dog, you could try kneeing him in the chest when he jumps on you. However, most of your visitors would not feel comfortable making this type of correction on your dog. It would be better to arm your guests with the spray bottle as they enter your home. Many dogs get over the excitement of visitors once they have been in the house for about half an hour. With this in mind, if Einstein is overpowering in his greeting of your guests, put him in his crate or ex-pen prior to their arrival, and let some time pass before you let him out to say hello. If you should elect to take this approach, have a marrowbone ready to give him when you lock him up. Many dogs resent guests coming over because it means they have to go to their crates. However, if you give him a new marrowbone he will probably prefer it to the guests, and there will be no resentment. When you let him out once the excitement is over, make him lie down by your chair, rather than allowing him to climb all over your visitors. (See Chapter 13.)

SILENCE IS GOLDEN

One other annoying habit is nuisance barking. There is a difference between the dog that barks to let you know that someone has arrived at your door and a dog that simply likes the sound of his own bark. Not only is nuisance barking annoying to you, it can be annoying to your neighbors as well. A dog that barks constantly inside the house makes for a poor watchdog. You become so conditioned to the barking that if something were to go on outside you would probably pay little attention. Ideally, your dog should alert you when all is not well and should be able to discriminate between things that go on in the neighborhood on a daily basis and things that are out of the ordinary.

If you have a dog that barks more than he should, you can start to teach him to be quiet with the use of lemon juice. Buy a plastic squeeze lemon at the grocery store. Attach the check cord to his collar. When Einstein starts to bark, first step on the check cord so he cannot run off. Next, tell him, "Quiet!" If he persists in barking tell him, "Quiet!" a second time, but then open his mouth and give him a good squirt of lemon juice. In order for Einstein to get rid of the taste of the lemon, he will have to lick, swallow, and salivate. While he is doing this, he will be unable to bark. Since he is being quiet, you should be praising him. Remove your foot from the check cord and allow him to leave. Each time he barks unnecessarily, repeat the procedure. Follow the same guidelines when he is outdoors, too. Never call him to you to correct him. Always go out and step on the check cord. Then make your correction. If the lemon juice is not effective, then you may need to invest in a no-bark collar. (See Chapter 15.)

CHAPTER 10

Introducing Your Puppy to Other Furry and Feathered Friends

HE AIN'T NOTHIN' BUT A HOUND DOG

If you have another dog at home, you need to consider the best way to introduce him to the new puppy. Some dogs, like children, are thrilled when you come home with a little brother or sister,

◀ Even a dog-friendly cat may take time to adjust to a new puppy. U-CD, Ch. Goose Creek Commentator CDX, NA, CGC, owned by "Mike" Walters-Williquette. *Photo by "Mike" Walters-Williquette. Petit Basset Griffon Vendeen, Hound Group.*

while others are jealous of the new arrival. If your older dog is large, then he could accidentally injure Einstein when they play. If he is small then Einstein may possibility injure him. If you have a dog that would prefer not to have a brother or sister, then he might injure your puppy intentionally. Rather than find out the hard way whether the two dogs are compatible, the best solution is to keep them separated until Einstein is a little older and bigger. Give the dogs a chance to meet when Einstein is behind the baby gate or in the ex-pen. If that is not possible then be sure that both dogs are on leash and under control when they meet for the first time. Some people prefer to introduce the dogs on neutral territory. This may be the answer when you introduce another adult dog to your home, but I think it a waste of time to do this with a puppy. Most dogs do not perceive a puppy as an adversary. In addition, you may have difficulty finding an area that would be safe for your puppy to visit. You should not take him to a park or school grounds until he has had several inoculations. You do not know the health of the dogs that have recently visited the site.

When you finally allow the two dogs to meet nose to nose, be sure to stay with them in case there is a problem. If your adult dog is tolerant of the puppy, then allow them to play for a while before you put Einstein back in his den. Some puppies torture an older dog by playing too rough, and many older dogs may be more tolerant of a puppy's behavior than they should be. Some puppies never stop playing and exhaust an older dog. It is up to you to make sure your older dog gets some peace and quiet. Furthermore, when you have to go off and leave Einstein alone, do not leave him in the company of the older dog, no matter how well they get along. Your puppy needs some rest, as does your older dog—so separate them.

WHAT'S NEW, PUSSYCAT?

If you have a resident cat, you must be very careful when you introduce a canine into a feline household. Some cats never accept a new puppy or dog, even if they were once raised with one. Fortunately, cats can usually get away from a dog if they need to, by jumping out of reach. Even a dog-friendly cat may take time to adjust to a new puppy, while a predatory cat may consider Einstein something you conveniently brought home for his dinner! If you have not had Morris, your cat, de-clawed then you must protect Einstein from being scratched. For safety's sake, have your cat's claws clipped before you even bring Einstein through the door. As an alternative, you can place specially designed plastic caps over your cat's claws. Puppies lead with their heads. If your cat stands his ground and your puppy approaches this new aberration too closely, the cat may lash out and scratch Einstein in the eye. At worst, this could cause him to go blind. Even if he is not physically hurt, a con-frontation with an adult cat can be frightening for a puppy that has had no experience with the outside world. A bad experience with Morris may make him hate cats for the rest of his life. Many cats will avoid a conflict with a dog, providing the dog does not invade their space. For that reason, allow the two to meet for the first time when Einstein is behind the baby gate or in the ex-pen.

If your cat is de-clawed, you may have to protect Morris from Einstein. Without claws, he will have no means of protecting him-self. Cats often like to torment dogs because they know they can usually get out of harm's way. If your cat is tormenting Einstein then you may need to confine Morris when Einstein is out of his crate. There will be plenty of time to let them get to know each other when Einstein is a little older, and wiser. In addition, when you leave Einstein alone, prevent Morris from being able to get into Einstein's den area. If Morris is sitting on the kitchen counter only a few inches away from the crate or ex-pen, Einstein may be barking for hours, out of frustration, while the cat deliberately torments him.

One complaint voiced by the owners of both dogs and cats is that the puppy chases the cat all over the house. This is often a game instigated by the cat and thoroughly enjoyed by the dog. This game of chase is often disruptive, and it is usually the puppy that gets into trouble, while nobody attaches blame to the cat. One of the best ways to control this situation is to attach a check cord to Einstein's collar. As he chases after the cat through the area in which he is allowed to roam, say, "No," "Quit," or something similar. Then step on the check cord as he goes running past you. He will come to a screeching halt! Continue to correct him in this manner until you can simply tell him to quit and he will do so. However, some dogs never do get over chasing, or herding, the cat.

LOW-FLY ZONE

Some people keep birds as pets. If Einstein is a "bird dog," it may be asking a lot for your puppy to let the bird alone. Instinct always overcomes training. If a bird resides in your house, you need to take similar precautions to those suggested for introducing Einstein to a cat. If you sometimes allow your bird to fly around in the house, then make sure you confine Einstein to his crate when this event occurs. Dogs will be dogs, and a bird flying just overhead may trigger that hunting instinct. Someone I know once had a mynah bird, which could talk up a storm and call the dogs by name. This person had several dogs, none of which ever showed much interest in the bird. One day, while the mynah bird was out of its cage and all the dogs were in the house, the bird came up missing. The bird's owner never did discover which dog had blackbird pie for supper.

If you have other pets, take similar precautions when introducing them to Einstein. Remember that at one time most dogs were hunters. This long-forgotten instinct may be lying dormant ready to surface at any moment. Dogs and cats can generally coexist without much problem, but dogs should never be left alone unsupervised with any other type of pet. When a dog kills a rabbit or a bird, he is only doing something quite natural for a dog.

CHAPTER 11

Latchkey Pups

In the past, women stayed home to raise the kids, and since they were home all day, the job of raising the family dog fell to them. Today, things have changed, and the majority of women work outside the home. Children spend their days at the day-care center or at school. Raising a puppy today is not as simple as it once was; therefore, what is the best way to raise Einstein if you work all day?

To begin, you will have to be prepared to make significant changes in your lifestyle when you come home from work. A puppy left alone all day will be eagerly awaiting your arrival after your day at the office. Although you may be tired from working, and from your commute, Einstein will be fully rested and ready to play. You cannot expect to come home, sit down, and relax in front of the TV as you have done in the past. Instead, you will need to take Einstein for a long walk or play fetch in the backyard for some

◄ Even for people who work full time, schedules can be adjusted to successfully raise a puppy. Litter of Crisam's Miniature Schnauzers, breeder Christine E. Haycock FPSA. *Photo by Christine E. Haycock FPSA. Miniature Schnauzers, Terrier Group.*

considerable time. After you both have eaten dinner, be prepared to give Einstein more exercise. Remember that a good dog is a tired dog.

You will also have to decide on the best way to house-train Einstein when you are not around to take him out to relieve himself. With a little planning, you should be able to come up with a way to do this successfully. There are several options open to you.

If you have a spouse or partner, consider the following course of action. Determine if you both can modify your work schedules for the next few months so that Einstein does not have to spend quite so many hours at home by himself. Maybe one of you could go to work much earlier than usual, which would enable you to return home early. In turn, the other family member could go in to work later and come home later. This would minimize the number of hours Einstein would have to remain alone. Another possibility would be for one of you to take a longer lunch break and come home on your lunch hour. Some businesses allow their employees to select their working hours, just as long as they do their jobs. A puppy can tolerate spending up to five hours in a crate; otherwise he should be left in an ex-pen or kennel run.

If you live in a temperate climate and have a vehicle large enough to accommodate your crate, you might be able to take Einstein to work with you and leave him in the vehicle. Then, instead of taking a coffee break mid-morning, you can take a puppy break. You can also pack a lunch each day and spend your lunch hour at the park with Einstein. The exercise you get during your lunch break will be good for you both. Taking Einstein to work is only possible if you have a place to keep your vehicle out of the sun or, in the case of the northern climates, a location where your puppy will not freeze. (See Chapter 16, "Going Along for the Ride.") Some understanding employers allow staff to bring a young puppy into the office, provided the puppy remains in his crate and does not cause a disturbance.

Do you have a trustworthy neighbor whom you can pay to come in several times a day to let Einstein out and then play with him for a few minutes? Perhaps you know a stay-at-home mom or dad or a retired person who would appreciate a little extra cash.

Check with your local kennel. Does it offer puppy day-care? Some kennels understand how difficult it is for working families to raise a puppy successfully, and they offer this service. When you leave Einstein at puppy day-care, he will have the opportunity to play with other puppies of similar ages. The kennel staff can also let him out whenever he needs to relieve himself.

If none of these suggestions is possible, then you will need to consider how you are going to housebreak Einstein when you leave him home alone. This will not be an easy task. Leaving a puppy alone in a crate for more than five hours is unfair, and guaranteed to teach him to soil his den. As you learned in Chapter 9, dogs do not like to soil their dens, but sometimes the owner leaves them little choice.

If you have a medium to small breed, you might try placing a large cat-litter box in the corner of the ex-pen and filling it with "clumping" cat litter. For several days, place Einstein in the litter box after you feed him and encourage him to relieve himself in it. Then, when you are at work he will have a special place to eliminate if he needs to do so.

Some owners of more mature dogs are reluctant to leave their dogs access to the outside while they are away. Although these dogs are totally housebroken and trustworthy in the house, their owners understand the need for their dogs to relieve themselves while they are gone. Although they expect to get home by 6 p.m. they might suddenly be faced with overtime or become held up in traffic. A dog can only cross his legs for so long. One of my friends solved this concern by turning part of her garage into her dog's potty area, in case of this eventuality. First, she installed a doggie door in the door leading from the house to the garage so her dog could get out of the house if necessary. Next, she sectioned off a small part of the garage by making a box out of 1″ × 8″ boards, standing on edge. She placed a heavy, plastic drop cloth on the floor, and then covered it with cedar shavings that she bought at a pet supply house. These shaving are normally used in small animal cages. Finally, she placed an ex-pen around the boards so her dog could not reach other areas of the garage. By containing her dog within this pen, she solved two additional problems. The fence prevented Shorty from being hit by the vehicle when she drove into the garage, and in addition, it stopped him from running out into the street when the overhead garage door was raised. If you elect to go this route, you will need to teach Einstein to eliminate in that area.

You can modify this idea to serve a puppy. You could handle it in one of two ways. You could set up a pen in the garage, filled with cedar shavings. You could then place Einstein's crate at one end to give him both a sleeping place and a potty area. Alternatively, if you have a doggie door between the house and garage, you could put his crate or another ex-pen inside the house immediately in front of the dog door. This way, Einstein can leave the indoor area to relieve himself but not have access to the rest of the house. If you choose this method, be sure to anchor the inside crate or ex-pen to the area of the dog door so that Einstein cannot get loose in the house.

If you live in an apartment or condominium, you will not be able to use the above idea unless you have a garage attached to your unit. However, if you have a smaller breed you could purchase a child's plastic wading pool and fill it with shredded newspaper. The plastic from which the pool is constructed will prevent urine from penetrating the floor of the apartment. The eight-inch sides of the pool will prevent the paper or shavings, if you decide to use them, from spilling all over the floor. You can place your ex-pen around the pool.

If you allow your puppy the freedom of your fenced yard while you are gone, he is bound to get into all kinds of mischief. He may eat rocks, chew on shrubbery, and dig holes everywhere. Although your yard is fenced, consider buying a freestanding kennel run in which to house Einstein while you are away. Be sure to place the run in a shady location, or if that is out of the question, place a shade cloth on the top and sides to protect him from the sun. Give him a dry place to go in case of inclement weather and make sure he has a water bucket in the run with him.

Although Einstein has access to a potty area, indoors or out, when you are away, when you return home, you must immediately take Einstein out to relieve himself. Because many dogs are so clean, they do not like to soil their area unless they absolutely have to. However, the unwitting owner believes that because their dog had access to a potty area while they were gone all day, it is not necessary to exercise Einstein the minute they arrive home. Instead, they immediately let him into the house, and guess what happens next—once released from his confinement Einstein soils the floor.

If you have a latchkey child, as well as a latchkey puppy, you must instruct your child what to do when he comes home from school. You cannot expect young children to take full responsibility for caring for a puppy. Your child might be responsible enough to let Einstein out to relieve himself, but depending on the age of the child Einstein may need to be put back in his crate or run, until you get home from work. Children quickly forget to watch a puppy in their charge, and the puppy in turn can get into trouble when unsupervised in the house.

Most puppies need to eat three times a day until they are three months old. Then they can be moved to two meals a day. It may be difficult to feed Einstein more than twice a day if there is nobody coming to look after him while you are gone. If this is the case, you have several choices. You can feed him only twice a day and continue this schedule on the weekends. You can place him on a self-feeding program, which may make housebreaking more difficult. Finally, you can invest in a feeder that is on a timer. When the clock reaches the hour at which you want Einstein fed, the lid to the container will open, allowing your puppy to get his meal.

CHAPTER 12

Starting Off on the Right Paw

In addition to teaching Einstein social graces, you must teach him to obey some commands, both for his personal safety and for your convenience. Ask one hundred dog owners, "What is the most important command your dog can learn?" and the reply will be unanimous—"To come when called."

HOW PUPPIES LEARN

Before you teach Einstein to obey commands, you first need to understand how a dog learns. When your dog does things you like or dislike, you need to inform him that his actions meet with your approval or disapproval. He receives this information in the form of verbal praise, through the use of food or toys, and by verbal or

◀ It is never too early to start teaching your puppy to come when called. *Photo by Nelson Enochs. Border Collie, Herding Group.*

119

even physical correction, if necessary. Physical correction does not mean a beating. If you catch Einstein soiling the floor you might scold him by saying, "No, bad boy. Get outside," as you grab him by the collar and propel him through the door into the yard. Your tone of voice gives him information that he has just made a mistake. In this case, he selected an inappropriate location in which to eliminate. Furthermore, you physically corrected him by first grabbing him by his collar and then by taking him unceremoniously out the door. It should have left no room for doubt in his mind that he did something wrong when you treated him in this manner. Once outside, if he resumed eliminating then you should say in a happy tone of voice, "That's it, good boy. Go potty," while at the same time you reach in your pocket and reward him with a treat. This time he learned by your actions that he did the right thing.

The timing of your praise and correction must coincide with whatever your dog is doing at the time, in order for it have any meaning. (See Chapter 21, the story about Squeaky.) In order to make it clear how easy it is to praise your dog for the wrong thing, we can take another example of housebreaking. One bitterly cold day, rather than don a snowsuit and go outdoors with Einstein, you turn him outside by himself so that he can do his business. By reading Chapter 9 you know that you must make sure he does his business before you let him back inside, so you take up a post by the window where you can observe what he is doing. Once you have seen that he has finished eliminating, you go to the door to let him back inside. In the meantime, Einstein is anxious to get back in the warm house and is leaping against the door to draw your attention to the fact that his paws are cold. As you reach the door you tell him how pleased you are that he did his business outside, cold as it might be. From the other side of the door he hears you saying, "Oh, what a good boy you are," as he is in mid-leap. Consequently, he says to himself, "Wow, she likes me jumping on the door. She just told me so." Therefore, the next time you allow him to go outside without you, he may jump up on the door again, to let you know that it is time to bring him in.

Conversely, on a warm summer day Einstein is enjoying some fresh air and exercise in the backyard while you sit in the air conditioning. You happen to glance out of the same window and notice Einstein digging in the cool dirt of the flower beds. You go rushing to the door to reprimand him while, during that time, Einstein has wandered off to his spot, where he is starting to eliminate. You come flying through the door yelling, "You bad dog. Get out of there!" Poor Einstein is going to shake his head in confusion. For weeks you have been telling him to "Go potty" in that spot, and now you are yelling at him. No wonder he is bewildered by your actions.

As you can see from these two examples, timing is everything when it comes to training a puppy. Furthermore, the tone of voice that you use has more meaning than the words you say. A happy tone tells the dog he is right, a gruff tone tells the dog he is wrong, and a tone used with authority says you are serious. Puppies, and for that matter dogs, do not understand English, or any other language for that matter. Instead, they learn sounds. Commands should be short words, not long sentences, so that is why we use such commands as sit, down, and come.

TEACHING YOUR DOG BY USING LURES AND REWARDS

When it comes to training your puppy, you will be more successful if you use lures and rewards when introducing Einstein to commands. When you introduce a dog to a command, you lure him into doing what you want. Dogs learn faster, and enjoy their training more, if you use positive reinforcement. When you use a lure, which usually consists of food or a toy, your puppy is subjected to positive reinforcement. A simplified explanation follows. You hold the lure in front of your puppy's nose and move it in the direction you want the dog to go. Your dog gets to eat the treat or play with the toy when he makes the correct response. However, you use a lure only in the teaching phase. After a number of repetitions of the command that you are introducing, you remove the lure. This could be after several training sessions, or several weeks, depending on your dog's response to learning. There is no set time in which a puppy learns a command. Some puppies pick up training much faster than others do. Once you remove the lure, then Einstein is rewarded for correct response. The point at which you move from lure to reward is where many people go wrong. They never move beyond the lure part of their training.

When you use a reward, you give your puppy information that he obeyed correctly. In addition, you also need to let your dog know when he has done something wrong. This is when a correction comes into play. Unfortunately, some trainers mistakenly believe that any form of correction is wrong. Nonetheless, a correction also gives the dog information—that you are not pleased by his action. If you think your dog knows a command and chooses not to respond, you may need to correct him. This is the only way he will understand when he is right and when he is wrong. Just remember that a correction does not have to be harsh in nature. Moreover, teaching most dogs to respond to commands takes longer than you think, so if your puppy is not responding like you expect, consider that he may not fully understand the command.

HOW SHORT-TERM AND LONG-TERM MEMORY PLAY A PART IN TRAINING

When you first introduce Einstein to any command, or even to social graces, what you teach him initially only goes into short-term memory. The best way to explain this phenomenon is to compare short-term memory with a telephone number. If a number you call frequently changes suddenly, the next few times that you dial the number you will have to look it up. After you have called the new number several times, you will probably be able to recall the first three digits. Then, after you dial the number a few more times you may remember the other four digits, but not necessarily in the correct order. Eventually, after you have dialed the number on several more occasions, you will no longer have to look it up because it will have moved into your long-term memory.

This is the same way a dog absorbs commands. At first, it will appear that you are starting from scratch with every training session. Although Einstein appeared to be catching on to what you wanted during a previous training session, when you start to work with him at the next session it will seem as if he has forgotten everything he had previously learned. Then one day the light will go on. This is the moment when the command you were teaching him moves into long-term memory.

To Come or Not to Come, That Is the Question

So many dog owners tell me that their dogs know the command "come" but they choose to ignore the command. I always ask them how much training their dogs have received on this command. I ask them at what age they started teaching their dogs what "come" meant, how many times a day they took their dogs out to practice, and for how long. The response I usually get is "Oh, I never really taught him, but he knows what I mean because he comes once in a while when he feels like it." In your case, from the day you bring Einstein home you are going to teach him what "come" means.

First, choose the command you are going to use—"come" or "here" will do. It does not matter what you use as long as you always use the same word every time. When he is very young Einstein will most likely come whenever you speak to him, even if you happen to say, "Bananas." The reason he does is because he feels insecure, but this phase will not last long! Always keep some treats or a toy in your pocket so that you can reward him for his response, or lure him into coming to you if necessary.

MAKING "COME" POSITIVE

Whenever Einstein is heading toward you, whether you spoke to him first or not say, "come." Squat down, hold out your hand, and as he is approaching, tell him how good he is. (See Figure 12-1.) When he reaches you, give him a treat or throw the toy for him to chase. Get down to his level so that you do not appear threatening.

Figure 12-1. Calling a puppy using a lure. *Photo by Shary Singer.*

Giving the command while Einstein is already doing what you want is similar to the way you introduce the command for potty training. When you see Einstein sniffing and circling in his spot you say, "Go potty, go potty, good boy." Eventually, he will come to associate the command with the action of relieving himself. Ultimately, in the case of "come" you will have to teach him that he has no choice in the matter, but in the beginning keep everything positive.

NEVER CORRECT YOUR PUPPY FOR COMING TO YOU

One thing you must consider when telling your puppy to come is that you must never call him to you if you need to correct him. If you catch him piddling on the rug and he runs off at your approach, never call him back to you. If you call him he might think that you are going to correct him and therefore refuse to obey. Every time you call your puppy, you must make it a positive experience. However, whether it is positive depends on Einstein's outlook. While a Labrador might enjoy getting a bath, a Beagle might hate it, so never call a puppy to you if you think he may perceive the end result as something unpleasant, like getting a bath. If you think your dog might not like what is about to happen to him when he reaches you, then go and get him rather than utter the command, "Come." This is why you should select a specific command for sending Einstein into his crate or ex-pen. (See Chapter 13.) Never tell him to come and then lock him up. You may see no reason for him to dislike going in his kennel, but he may not be ready for bed. Therefore, when the time comes to confine Einstein use the word "kennel," "bed," "house," or something along those lines, rather than saying, "Come."

THE SERIOUS SIDE OF "COME"

As Einstein gets older, and more confident, you will notice he is becoming increasingly independent. If you tell him to come and he chooses to ignore you, then that is the time to place the check cord on his collar so that he has no choice in the matter. Remember, coming when called is never optional. Hold the end of the check cord so that you can prevent him from leaving if he so desires. Extend your hand toward him and show him the lure. Then tell him to come while you move backward, away from him. If he comes toward you, verbally praise him while, at the same time, drawing your hand toward your body until it is close to your legs. When he reaches your hand, give him the lure. You did this in the past, but at that time, he was coming to you willingly.

You are going to work for several days in this manner, both inside and outdoors. Select a treat that Einstein finds irresistible, or use his favorite toy as the lure. You want him to be keen to reach you when you call him. If he ever chooses not to respond, you have a means of making him since he is wearing a check cord. If you tell him, "Come" and he stands and looks at you or turns to head off in another direction, then tug on the check cord while repeating the command "Come" to bring him toward you. Once he gets to you, reward him with his treat or toy. Moreover, don't forget to give him verbal praise as well.

Once Einstein is responding well to "come," and you believe that he understands what you want, then remove the lure and simply reward him for coming instead. Instead of extending your hand, keep it at your side when you tell him to come. Continue to praise him as he approaches you. Once he has reached you, reward him with the treat or toy. The only difference you have made is that you are no longer luring him to you. You continue to reward him for the correct response to "come."

During this learning stage, Einstein is certainly going to make the mistake of not coming when you call him. You want this to happen because he must understand there are consequences if he does not come. Allow him to run around with the check cord dragging behind him. Tell him to come, and reward him for the correct response. However, if he continues on his merry way, or simply ignores you, do not repeat the command to come but take off after him, until you can step on the check cord. Once you have snagged him, pick up the cord, give it a firm yank, and repeat the command "come" in a determined voice. Once Einstein reaches you, change your tone of voice to your praise tone, and reward him for coming. You must practice "come" on a daily basis, as many times as you can, both indoors and out. If you purchased a retractable leash as part of your puppy starter kit (Chapter 7), alternate by using it and the check cord, when you practice outside. Allow Einstein to scamper about with the leash retracting and extending. Then suddenly, when he is not paying attention to you, tell him, "Come." If Einstein fails to respond, engage the "brake" on the Flexi®. The moment the leash has stopped his forward motion, extend your arm toward him and then pull the leash toward you and release the brake. If he starts moving in your direction, begin to praise him. If he simply stands there, then engage the brake again, and repeat the same procedure. The use of the Flexi® gives Einstein immediate feedback. He hears your command to come, and if he does not respond instantly, he is prevented from running any farther by a jerk on his collar. However, dogs quickly learn to watch for you holding onto a leash, so that is why you alternate the retractable with the trailing check cord. The Flexi® makes an instant correction, but a dog will sometimes learn to avoid a correction by responding immediately if he knows you have the leash in your hand. If this is the case with Einstein, then when he is running around trailing a check cord, call him at a time when you can immediately step on the cord if he ignores your call. Stepping on the cord will work in a similar manner to using the brake on the Flexi®.

A word of warning with the use of a retractable leash: Occasionally, you may not be gripping the handle of the retractable leash firmly enough, and it could be pulled out of your hand as you engage the brake. Since the retractable leash is attached to your puppy's collar, its hard case will then be dragging close behind Einstein and may cause him to run off in panic. To prepare Einstein for this eventuality, put him on a regular leash, and then set the brake of the retractable so that the case is locked about eight feet from the snap of the leash. Attach it to Einstein's collar and then walk him around, holding onto his regular leash while the case of the retractable drags eight feet behind him. Once he has become accustomed to this, gradually move the case closer to Einstein until he ignores it. Many dogs begin to enjoy this new "game" and turn around and start to play with the case.

If you have young children, do not allow them to take Einstein out on a retractable leash. It requires considerable hand-to-dog coordination, which they will not have. It also allows a puppy a lot of freedom, and it can easily tangle around objects in Einstein's path. Children may not be as observant as you might be of potential hazards out-of-doors. In addition, the cord of most retractable leashes is light in weight and easily chewed. Therefore, keep a retractable for adult use and allow the children to walk Einstein on a regular leash.

GAMES PEOPLE PLAY

As long as there is at least one family member to work with, from the day you bring Einstein home you can turn teaching the word "come" into a game. Einstein must be wearing a check cord or leash in order to participate. The players each hold treats in their hands, and one person holds onto Einstein. Another member of the party extends his hand in the direction of Einstein and calls the puppy to him (See Figure 12-2.) In the beginning, the person calling Einstein will be squatting only a few feet away. As soon as the puppy reaches the caller, Einstein will be rewarded with a treat. Then the caller will catch hold of the check cord so that Einstein cannot leave the area. Another member of the group then calls Einstein and rewards him in like manner. As the puppy catches onto the game, the players can spread out a little so that Einstein has to run farther to get his reward. In addition to teaching Einstein what "come" means, this is a wonderful way of giving him some exercise. Before long, Einstein will catch onto the game so well that he will try to grab his treat and then take off to the next player. This is one reason why he must be wearing the check cord. You do not want him leaving the person who has just called him

Figure 12-2. Calling a puppy between two people. *Photo by Nelson Enochs.*

until someone else calls. The other reason for Einstein to wear a check cord is so that if he decides not to go to the person calling him, that person can make him do so. Over time, the players will be able to stand in the far reaches of the yard and still be able to call Einstein to them. The farther he has to run, the more exercise he will get. Do not forget that a good dog is a tired dog! With more training, you can turn this into a game of hide-and-seek that can be played either in the yard or in the house. One person holds Einstein while another goes off and hides. This will give Einstein a chance to test his olfactory powers. He will run to the area from which the sound is coming. Then he will have to search further, using his nose in order to find the player.

Another way of making "come" enjoyable also requires the participation of someone else in order to play the game. Most puppies are anxious to eat when feeding time rolls around. So, when you fix Einstein his meal, have someone hold him while you walk off with his meal. When they hear you call him to come, have that person release him so he can run to get his food.

KEEP HIM GUESSING

One mistake many dog owners make is to call their dogs to them only when they need them to come and at no other time. This is often when they are ready to leave for work, when they are ready for bed, or when it is time to leave the park. Their dogs quickly decide that to go to their owners when called is definitely not in their own best interest because it means their fun is about to end. Make it a practice around the house to call Einstein to you when you do not really need him to come. All you are going to do is reward him for coming and then let him go about his business. When you are home and Einstein is running around in the backyard, go to the door and call him to you. When he reaches the door, praise him, give him a treat, and then allow him to go back to play. Do this a number of times throughout the day.

When Einstein is totally reliable about coming whenever you call him, and will also respond to other family members, you need to slowly withdraw the food or toy rewards. However, you will continue to tell him that he is doing the right thing whenever he responds to your call, and you will pet him when he reaches you. When you begin to withdraw the food or toy reward, you will continue to give Einstein a reward at random. Always keep him guessing. Make him think that perhaps this time he is going to get something special. In fact, when you put him on a schedule of random reinforcement (giving him a reward occasionally) when you give him a treat for coming when called, give him several pieces all at one time. This is called a jackpot, and dogs work especially hard when a jackpot is involved.

Because coming when called is such an important command for any dog to learn, do not be in too great a hurry to eliminate the treats. You can withdraw them sooner when you teach other commands, but you want to make Einstein think that coming to you is really to his benefit, so always have a few treats in your pocket. Also, make sure other family members get the same response from Einstein when they call him. If Einstein ever gets out of the yard when you are not around, it is essential that he responds to whoever calls him.

CHAPTER 13

What Every Good Dog Should Know

While "come" may be the most important command you can teach your puppy, there are several other commands to which Einstein should learn to respond. No matter which command you teach him, the learning process will remain the same: repetition, short-term then long-term memory, and the use of lures and rewards. You can introduce the commands, "kennel" and "sit" as soon as Einstein has become acclimated to your home. However, delay introducing the commands of "down," "stay," "wait," "leave it," and "heel" until he is beginning to understand the others.

◀ Puppy interaction is a great way to remind Einstein of his roots—that he is, after all, canine. *Photo by Margret Taylor. Belgian Tervuren, Herding Group (left); Greater Swiss Mountain Dog, Working Group (right).*

THE "KENNEL" COMMAND

MAKING IT FUN

The first command that you should introduce to Einstein, aside from teaching him the command "come" is "kennel," "bed," "house," or whatever name you have chosen to use for his den. You want Einstein to understand that the command "kennel" does not mean the same thing as come. Every time you put Einstein into his den, say, "Kennel." You can lure him into his den by tossing a toy, marrowbone, or treat through the entrance. As he enters, tell him that he is a good boy. In the beginning, make teaching "kennel" into a game. Toss a tasty morsel into the back of the kennel or ex-pen so Einstein has to go completely into the crate or ex-pen to reach the lure. Once he has eaten the treat, let him back out, and then repeat the exercise. After a few weeks, you should expect him to go in the kennel on command, not only because you are using a lure.

KENNEL ON COMMAND

To teach "kennel," position Einstein immediately in front of the kennel, holding onto his check cord. Have a treat in your hand ready to reward him the moment he enters his den. Say, "kennel," and once he enters, reward him and then let him back out. If he chooses not to respond, repeat the command with a firm voice, and at the same time use the check cord to make him go in. Once he does so praise and reward him, and then let him back out. Repeat this until he instantly responds when he hears you say, "Kennel." Gradually move him farther from the kennel entrance so that he has to travel some distance after you issue the command. When you train him in this manner, by telling him, "Kennel" and then allowing him to come back out again, he will never know for sure whether you plan on keeping him in there or not. This way he should be less reluctant to enter the crate.

THE "SIT" COMMAND

"Sit" is another command Einstein should learn, and it is such an easy command to teach that he should learn it faster than any other one. Hold a lure in one hand, just above Einstein's head, centered between his eyes and his nose. Next, as you say, "Sit," move your hand back toward his tail (See Figure 13-1.) Because of the way dogs are built, as he raises his head, his rear will go down. (See Figure 13-2.) The moment his rear touches the floor, verbally praise him and give him the lure. When you teach sit, be sure you do not hold the lure too high above his head. Should you do so you will encourage Einstein to jump up to try to reach it. Repeat

Figure 13-1. The "sit" using a lure. *Photo by Shary Singer.*

Figure 13-2. Puppy receives food and praise. *Photo by Shary Singer.*

sit several times, then quit for the session. Puppies have a short attention span, and you should stop any training before they become bored with learning.

If Einstein is not interested in the lure, how do you get him to sit? You use an old-fashioned method: You place him in the position and then reward him with praise and a treat if he will eat one. Hold onto his collar with your right hand, say, "Sit," and gently press down on his rump with your left hand. (See Figures 13-3A and 13-3B.)

You will be surprised at how quickly Einstein catches on to "sit" when you use a lure. When you believe he understands what "sit" means, remove the lure as you did when you taught the commands

A

B

Figures 13-3A & 13-3B. Teaching the "sit" without using a lure. *Photo by Nelson Enochs.*

"come" and "kennel." Put your check cord on Einstein. With your hands at your side while holding a hidden treat, tell him to sit. If he sits, reward him with the food or toy. If he ignores you, then you are going to correct him gently. Hold the check cord in your right hand, close to his collar, and tell him to sit. If he obeys, reward him. If he ignores you as he likely will, tap him gently on his rump with the fingers of your left hand. The moment his rear touches the ground, praise and reward him with his treat or toy. Repeat this until you no longer have to tap him on the rear to make him sit. Then put him on a schedule of random reinforcement as explained in Chapter 12.

THE "LIE DOWN" COMMAND

"Sit" is not such a useful command as "down." When a dog is relaxing he usually lies down, rather than sitting. Therefore, if you ever need Einstein to stay in one place for any length of time, always have him lie down. Some dogs consider "down" a position of submission. Therefore, if Einstein is on the dominant side, you may have a battle ahead of you. From experience I have found the terrier breeds among the most difficult to teach to respond to the "down" command. You will teach your puppy "down" once you have him sitting. There is a good reason for this. When Einstein is sitting, he is already halfway there. His rear is already where you want it to be, so all you have to do is concentrate on his front.

Put the check cord or a leash on Einstein and have him sit next to you, on your left. Place your left hand on his neck, slipping your thumb under his collar with your fingers spreading across his shoulders. (See Figure 13-4.) Hold the lure in your right hand immediately in front of his nose. Tell him, "Down," and at the same time lower the lure towards the ground while you put pressure on his shoulders with your left hand. (See Figures 13-5 and 13-6.) The moment his chest touches the floor, praise him and allow him to eat the treat or take hold of the toy. Do not try to make him stay in that position. Allow him to get up if he wishes. As with teaching the "sit," practice the "down" a few times, and then quit.

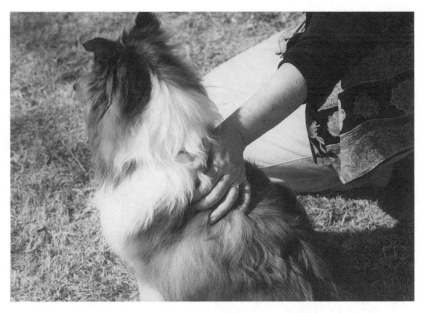

Figure 13-4. Close-up showing correct hand placement on puppy's shoulder for the "down." *Photo by Shary Singer.*

Figure 13-5. Teaching the "down" using a lure. *Photo by Shary Singer.*

Figure 13-6. Close-up showing correct hand placement on puppy's shoulder and correct position of the lure. *Photo by Shary Singer.*

What do you do if Einstein wants to do battle or simply will not cooperate? There are several solutions from which to choose. When you tell him, "down" and he balks, grasp his collar with your left hand while you slide your right arm under his chest and lift his legs out from underneath him. (See Figure 13-7.) Gently lay him on the ground. (See Figure 13-8.) As an alternative, you can reach over his back with your left hand and grasp his outside leg just below the elbow. At the same time you can grasp his inside leg in the same manner with your right hand, raise him into a begging position, and then lower him to the ground. (See Figure 13-9.) You may need to put pressure on his shoulders with your left arm as you lower him to the ground.

Sometimes you can take a small puppy by surprise by picking him up and cuddling him to get him to relax. Then, when he is lying in your arms you can lower him to the ground and get him lying down before he realizes what has happened. Teaching your puppy

▲ Step 1.

▼ Step 2.

Figures 13-7 & 13-8. Teaching the "down" without the use of the lure, Steps 1 and 2. *Photo by Nelson Enochs.*

Figure 13-9. Teaching the "down" without the use of the lure, Step 3. *Photo by Nelson Enochs.*

to lie down may take several days, depending on how determined he is not to do so.

Once Einstein is lying down without a fight, then you need to insist that he remain lying down for several seconds. After you have rewarded him, hold onto his collar and, with pressure from your hand on his shoulders, keep him lying down for five seconds. While he is lying there, give him information that he is doing what you want by quietly praising him, and telling him what a good boy he is. Each time you make him lie down, gradually increase the length of time that he will remain lying on the ground without trying to get up. When he will remain lying down without a struggle for up to a minute, then place your foot on the check cord or leash, close to his collar. This will enable you to stand up beside him while he remains lying down. When you place your foot on the leash in this manner, it will make it difficult for him to get up.

When you feel Einstein understands what the command means and does not resist lying down, then you remove the lure and reward him once he lies down on command. Have him sit on your left, and grasp the right side of his collar in your left hand. Hold the food or toy out of sight in your right hand. When you tell Einstein to "down," do not point at the ground with your hand. Remember that you are no longer using a lure and usually you keep the lure in your hand. At the same time as you tell Einstein to down, you are going to pull gently on his collar in the direction of the ground. Most dogs move away from pressure, so he should start to lie down. As he does so, start to praise him so that he knows he is doing what you want. The moment his chest touches the floor, reward him by producing the treat or his toy and then allow him to get up. After a few repetitions, you will probably discover you need to put very little pressure on his collar to make him lie down. Finally, hold the check cord instead of his collar. If you tell him, "Down," and he does not move, pull the check cord in the direction of the ground.

THE "STAY" COMMAND

"Stay" is the second most important command you will teach Einstein. "Stay" should mean "Do not move" to your dog. Once Einstein is reliable at sitting and lying down on command, you can begin to teach him what "stay" means. Have him sit beside you on your left. He should be wearing a regular leash when you introduce him to this command. You cannot lure him into staying, so hide his treat or toy. Put slight tension on the leash and collar to prevent him from getting up. (See Figure 13-10.) Say, "Stay," and then step around in front of Einstein to face him. Stand only a foot or two in front of him and count to five. (See Figure 13-11.) Then step back to his side.

During this time, do not pet him since physical contact may make him move, although you may tell him very quietly that he is being good. Once you get back to his side, pause momentarily before praising him, and then allow him to get up. You do not want him leaping up the moment you stand beside him. When you teach "stay," you work on duration first before you work on distance.

Figure 13-10. Introducing the "sit stay," Step 1. *Photo by Nelson Enochs.*

What this means is that you continue to stand immediately in front of Einstein while you increase the length of time he has to sit still. Be fair; you cannot expect a young puppy to sit still for more than half a minute until he is a little older.

If Einstein should get up as you move away from him, while you are facing him, or as you return to his side, let him know that he

Figure 13-11. Introducing the "sit stay," Step 2. *Photo by Nelson Enochs.*

made a mistake. Say, "No" or "Wrong" and pull up gently on the leash, which should make him sit once more. You may even need to tell him to sit again. Many dogs catch on to "stay" quickly, while others are antsy. A few become submissive when you work on "stay" and keep trying to lie down. If that is the case, practice the "down stay" rather than "sit stay." When Einstein can stay while you stand in front of him for up to half a minute, then back away one step. If he decides to move because you are farther away from him, say, "No" or "Wrong" and step toward him as you pull up gently on the leash.

Always return to his side to praise and release him from the "stay." Never call him to you. Why not? Because you are attempting to teach him that the command "stay" means "You do not move." Therefore do not confuse him by calling him to you. When Einstein no longer gets up when you are standing one giant step away from him, add another step. (See Figure 13-12.) If he con-

Figure 13-12. "Sit stay" with slack in the leash. *Photo by Nelson Enochs.*

tinues to stay, it is time to test him to see if he truly understands what the command means.

Turn his collar so that the snap of the leash is under his chin. When you leave his side, go about three feet away. After Einstein has stayed for about five seconds, gently pull on the leash in your direction. If you feel him resisting, quietly tell him how good he is. If you praise him with too much enthusiasm, he will most likely get up. If you see him leaning toward you or if he starts to get up, say, "No" or whatever word you use to let him know he is making a mistake. Once he is back sitting, then try the test again. Apply tension to the leash for a few seconds only, not for the entire time he is on the "stay." Test him several times before you return to his side. As he catches on to the test, gradually increase the tension that you are applying to his collar, until you can pull fairly hard. (See Figure 13-13.)

Once Einstein shows you he understands he is not to move when you apply tension to the leash, try this additional test. Tell him to stay and stand about four feet away, facing him. Make sure you have slack in the leash. Suddenly, step quickly right or left. Your fast movement may cause Einstein to get up. If he does, correct him, like you did for moving when you applied tension to the leash. Try it again. When Einstein continues to sit there when you step right or left, then jump instead. When he catches on to this new game, then suddenly squat down in front of him. Does he resist the urge to get up?

When Einstein can sit through all of these tests, then he understands what "sit stay" means. You can now repeat this training with him when he is in a "down" position. Remember that if you ever need to leave Einstein in one spot for very long, you would leave him in a "down," not in a "sit stay," so this is the "stay" position for you to perfect. If he tries to get up at any time on the "down," drop your hand onto his shoulder, tell him, "No" or "Wrong," and push him back into position. Do not pull up on the leash since that will cause him to sit. You can have Einstein remain on the "down stay" for longer than on the "sit stay." Build up the time slowly. Finally, test him to see if he understands that he must resist the urge to get up. Have him lie down, and then when he has stayed there

Figure 13-13. Puppy resisting the pull of the leash on a "sit stay." *Photo by Nelson Enochs.*

for several seconds, start to pull up on the leash in the same way that you pulled forward when he was on the "sit stay." He should resist the impulse to get up. (See Figure 13-14.) If he tries to sit up when he feels the upward tension on his collar, then immediately push on his shoulders with your left hand and tell him, quite firmly, to "down."

Figure 13-14. Puppy resisting sitting up on the "down stay." *Photo by Nelson Enochs.*

THE "WAIT" COMMAND

Many dogs get injured or even killed when they bolt out of the house when an outside door or gate to the yard is opened by someone going in or out. For safety's sake, you should teach your puppy not to rush through doors. Over the years, students have told me that teaching their puppies "door manners" is one of the most useful social graces their dogs learned. The best way to do so is through the use of negative reinforcement. Sometimes you need to do something negative to your dog now to avoid grief later.

The door you should use is your front door since this is where you are likely to have the most trouble. The front door is where the UPS driver delivers packages and where your guests arrive. This door normally leads to the street, where there is traffic. This door is the one that you most want your puppy to respect. If you have a screen door in addition to the front door, then prop the screen door open. Put Einstein on a regular leash and make sure it has plenty of slack. You do not want Einstein to realize that the leash is on, nor do you want him to get loose in the front of the house.

In this instance, his leash works like a safety-line. When you open the door, open it just wide enough to allow Einstein to barely run through. He is bound to try to go out of the door, and you will not try to prevent him from doing so. The moment his head and shoulders pass between the door and the frame, carefully squeeze the door against his body. (See Figures 13-15A and 13-15B.) You are not trying to hurt him. Instead, you are trying to show him that doors can sometimes close as he goes through them. As you hold the door against his body, say, "Wait, wait, wait," and then release the pressure of the door and use the leash to bring him back into the house.

Try it again. You may find Einstein wants no part of going through that door. Good! He has learned a valuable lesson. If you can only catch him once, then test him every day until he forgets the lesson, and you can catch him out again. If you have a fenced backyard with a gate to the front yard, test him in the same manner with the gate also. Occasionally, when you open any interior door in the house, try to catch him out. Never open a door wide if you are testing him. The wider you open the door, the harder you will have to close it to trap him. The idea is not to hurt Einstein but to make him cautious when approaching any door.

Once you have caught Einstein out the first time, if he stands back whenever you open the door, pass through it yourself and then call him to come through after you. Teach him that when you give him a command to go through the door, nothing is going to happen to him.

You might wonder why you do not use the command "stay" instead? Remember that you always return to your dog when you tell him to stay. If you say, "Stay" to Einstein and then do not invite him to go with you, do you really expect him to be in the same spot when you come home several hours later? Of course you do not; neither did you mean you wanted him to stay. All you wanted was to go through the door while he stayed on the other side. This is the reason we tell him to wait and not to stay.

When Einstein shows you that rushing doors is no longer a concern, you can make him wait before you let him out of the car. Do not ever consider trying to trap him with the car door—you could kill him. When you are in the car, keep him on leash. Open the car door, and as you do so, say, "Wait." If he attempts to get out before you do, jerk him back firmly with the leash and tell him to wait once more. Is this unfair? Many owners like to take their dogs for a ride in the car when they go to the grocery store. Unfortunately, the parking lot of the grocery store is where a number of dogs are killed or injured each year. When the owner opens the door of the vehicle to get out or to put groceries inside the vehicle, the dog leaps out and gets hit by a passing car. If you ever need to do anything negative to your puppy, always consider the consequences if you do not correct him. You will then feel better about doing it.

If you have a small dog, you may need to wait until he is older before teaching him to wait at the door. Using the door to trap a puppy of one of the smaller breeds may be risky. However, small dogs are usually more vulnerable than large dogs when it comes to being a highway statistic. Drivers can see a dog as large as a Labrador running toward the street, but a dog as small as a Yorkie is almost invisible to the driver in a car. Therefore, at some point you will need to teach your small dog that he must also wait at the door until invited through, but delay teaching this until he is bigger.

Figure 13-15A. Teaching "wait" at the door. *Photo by Nelson Enochs.*

Figure 13-15B. Dog trapped by the door. *Photo by Nelson Enochs.*

THE "LEAVE IT" COMMAND

The command "leave it" has many uses. One day you just might lose your grip on a chicken breast you are preparing for dinner and drop it right in front of Einstein, who has been waiting patiently for a handout. He will think that it must be his birthday as this large treat starts falling in his direction. However, a well-timed "leave it" command could save your dinner. If Einstein is playing ball with the children at the park, and the ball bounces into the street, a "leave it" command should stop your dog from following the ball and could possibly save his life.

As with training Einstein not to run out of the front door, the "leave it" command is taught in a negative manner. How can you lure a dog into leaving something he wants to get? Food works well for teaching this command. In addition, you will eventually reward him for leaving the food by then giving him a piece.

Place a piece of food between the tips of the fingers and thumb of one hand and hold your hand so the palm is facing you. (See Figure 13-16A.) When Einstein comes over to sniff your hand and try to grab the food, tell him, "Leave it." At the same time, flip the back of your hand toward him so that your knuckles rap him light-ly on his nose. (See Figure 13-16B.) He should be taken by sur-prise, but only momentarily. He will almost certainly try to reach for the food again. Repeat the same procedure. Most dogs when treated in this way will stand there, wondering what you are up to. When he has ignored whatever you have in your hand for several seconds, praise him and then tell him, "OK, get it," and offer him the treat. Continue to do this until when he starts to sniff your hand and you tell him to leave it, he will move his head away from your hand. Praise him, and then give him a treat with the command "get it."

There is an added advantage in teaching your dog the command "leave it." Some dogs like to snatch food from your hand and often come close to taking part of your fingers with it. By making your dog think he is about to get rapped on the nose by your knuckles, he is more likely to take his time in reaching for the food. In fact,

Figure 13-16A. Teaching your puppy not to grab food from your hand, Step 1. *Photo by Nelson Enochs.*

you can teach him the command "gently," once he has learned "leave it."

Once Einstein understands the command "leave it" when you are holding food, then you need to test him by putting food on the ground. In everyday life, you are more likely to need him to leave something that is lying on the ground. Perhaps you are on a walk in the park and he spots someone's discarded sandwich, or possibly he comes across a dead critter, which may make a delectable snack.

Figure 13-16B. Teaching your puppy not to grab food from your hand, Step 2. *Photo by Nelson Enochs.*

Prepare a plate with a few tasty morsels on it, and put Einstein on a check cord or leash. Place the plate on the ground, and then walk your puppy toward it. When he spots the goodies and moves ahead of you to help himself to a snack, tell him, "Leave it," and if he ignores you, give the leash a moderate jerk. (See Figures 13-17A and 13-17B.) Then tell him to leave it once more. When Einstein stops moving toward the plate of food anytime you tell him to leave it,

Figure 13-17A. Teaching your puppy to leave food dropped on the ground, Step 1. *Photo by Nelson Enochs.*

then take a piece of food off the plate and reward him with the treat. Hide a plate of treats somewhere in the yard and then go outside with Einstein, who is wearing his check cord. When he spots the plate give him a chance to go in that direction, then tell him, "Leave

Figure 13-17B. Teaching your puppy to leave food dropped on the ground, Step 2. *Photo by Nelson Enochs.*

it." Be prepared to step on the check cord to prevent him for getting to the plate if he does not stop when you tell him.

If your puppy is a ball fanatic, then teach him to leave the ball in a similar manner to the way you taught him to leave the food. Hold the ball in your hand, and if he tries to take it, pop him on the nose with the back of your hand. Once he only takes the ball when you tell him, "Get it," then lay the ball on the ground and walk him toward it like you did when there was food on the plate. Once he ignores the ball when you give him the command to leave it, then toss the ball, and as he runs after it, tell him to leave it. Ideally, you should be able to call him off the ball when you throw it. However, always reward him with a toss of the ball once he has left it when commanded.

Whenever corrections are introduced as part of a training approach, people sometimes feel uncomfortable about using them. They believe they are being cruel to their dogs and think there has to be another way to teach them. However, dogs do learn quickly with the use of negative reinforcement, just like a child who only touches a hot stove one time! By teaching your dog to respect doors and to leave a hazardous object on the ground, you may be being unkind for the moment, but Einstein should survive puppyhood. A dog that never learns these lessons may not himself survive.

THE "HEEL" COMMAND

Many people enjoy taking their dogs out for a walk, but it is not much fun if the dog takes you instead. If your small dog pulls on a leash, it is not a big deal, but if you own a larger dog then you need to teach him not to drag you along behind him. Never walk a larger dog with a harness. Sled dogs wear harnesses, and what do sled dogs do? They pull sleds!

You can teach your puppy to walk nicely on a leash in any number of ways. A lot depends on the type of puppy you own. If you have a puppy that likes to eat, you can use a food lure in the beginning. Hold a regular leash in your right hand so that it passes in front of your body. Hold a regular leash in your left hand and a treat in your right, just above Einstein's head. When he is focused on the treat, say, "Heel" or "Let's go" or even "Walkies," and start walking forward a few steps. If Einstein moves off with you, only travel a short distance before you allow him to get the lure. (See

Figure 13-18. Using a lure to teach your puppy to walk beside you. *Photo by Shary Singer.*

Figure 13-18.) Gradually increase the distance you walk before he receives his reward. Eventually you remove the lure and only reward him for his correct performance.

Dogs pull because they are eager to get somewhere. Therefore, another approach to teaching your dog not to pull on the leash is to stop moving forward whenever your puppy starts pulling. It may take several weeks to get the point across to Einstein, but this is a passive way of teaching your dog not to pull. At first, you may not travel far, but if you are patient and not looking for a lot of exercise then this might be the correct approach for you. Tell Einstein to heel as you start walking. As soon as he pulls hard on the leash, stop. When he finally comes back to your side to see what you are doing, say, "Heel" once more, and then repeat the procedure.

Another way to teach Einstein not to pull is more negative, but sometimes this is the fastest approach, particularly if you have a

Figure 13-19. The correct way to hold a leash when walking your puppy. *Photo by Nelson Enochs.*

strong or willful dog. With your dog on your left, place your right hand through the handle of the leash and your left hand on the leash some distance from the collar. (See Figure 13-19.) Tell him to heel and walk forward. As your puppy starts to pull on the leash, release

Figure 13-20A. Puppy starts to get ahead of the handler. *Photo by Nelson Enochs.*

your left hand from the leash (Figure 13-20A), turn quickly to your right, and begin walking briskly in the opposite direction. For a moment Einstein will feel slack in the leash, and then he will receive a jolt and will be stopped short. (See Figure 13-20B.) Look back over your shoulder and in a pleasant tone of voice say something like, "So, what happened to you? You weren't watching where I was going," and encourage him to catch up to you. (See Figure 13-

Figure 13-20B. Puppy receives jolt when he reaches the end of the leash. *Photo by Nelson Enochs.*

20C.) Because your tone of voice does not indicate that you are displeased with him, Einstein will think that he did this to himself. When he reaches you, stop and praise him and give him a treat.

Place your hands back on the leash as you did at the start, and begin walking again. Repeat the same procedure. After a few repetitions, you will notice that Einstein stops the moment he feels slack in the leash. When he does, praise him. At this point, you will

Figure 13-20C. Puppy turns to catch up with handler. *Photo by Nelson Enochs.*

no longer need to turn to go in the opposite direction. However, if he begins to fall back into old habits, then start turning and walking in the opposite direction once again.

THE DOG THAT WILL NOT WALK ON LEASH

Occasionally there is a dog that stubbornly refuses to walk on a leash. He simply sits there, no matter how much the owner cajoles.

One solution is to drive or carry the dog half a block away from your house. Then put him down and face him in the direction of home. Many dogs will walk toward the house even though they will not walk away from it. If this solution works for you, then increase the distance you take Einstein away from home before you put him down, and get him used to walking on leash.

Another trick is to find some loose gravel and place your puppy on it. Most puppies quickly figure out that if they balk on walking, it becomes most uncomfortable as they are dragged on the gravel. If you try this with Einstein, do not continue for very long if he refuses to budge. However, if he gets up on his feet and starts walking, praise and reward him and walk him onto grass or pavement as quickly as possible.

OFF TO SCHOOL

Although you may plan to do all your basic training at home, by yourself, it would be an excellent idea to enroll Einstein in a puppy training class, if one is available in your area. Each week most puppy training classes offer a period of socialization when the puppies get to play with each other. This puppy interaction is a great way for Einstein to be reminded of his roots, that he is, after all, canine. Puppies that attend puppy class are often more relaxed around other dogs when they get older. They have learned during class how to read canine body language. If you wait to take Einstein to class until he is older, it is doubtful that the dogs in class will be allowed to socialize. Some adolescent dogs are ready to do battle, and the instructor cannot afford to have that happen.

Another reason to enroll Einstein in puppy class is that he needs to respond to the commands he has learned in the presence of distractions. Aside from taking him to a Little League game, there will be little that is more distracting to Einstein than the presence of a bunch of other puppies. Moreover, competition between the owners to have the best dog in class is high, which assures that you will spend additional time training Einstein. With the name you have chosen, you need to prove that you do indeed have the smartest dog in class!

CHAPTER 14

Putting It All into Practice

In order to give Einstein more practice in the commands you are teaching him, consider how you might use some of them in everyday life. First, you must find out how reliable he really is on "come" when called. Dogs that come on command at home may not necessarily come when called in a strange place. There may simply be too much going on. Sometimes it is difficult to find a secure place to take your puppy off leash, (he should be wearing a check cord) and many communities have leash laws that preclude that altogether. In order to "test" Einstein, two places come to mind that are secure, although it is quite possible that there will be on display one of those nasty signs that says "No Dogs Allowed." Tennis courts and school yards are usually surrounded by fences, which will prevent a loose dog from coming into the area and Einstein from leaving.

◀ Ask friends or co-workers if they have a fenced yard that you could use to test Einstein's response to "come." *Photo by Margret Taylor. Golden Retrievers, Sporting Group.*

If you cannot use these facilities, ask a friend or co-worker if he has a fenced yard that you might use to test Einstein's response to "come." If you do use his yard, be a good dog neighbor. Exercise Einstein before you take him to your friend's home and pick up any pile Einstein may leave behind. Give Einstein as many experiences as possible off leash in strange locations, providing they are secure. Do remember that some breeds can never be trusted off the leash no matter how much training they have received.

In Chapter 9 you learned that puppies do not understand the difference between a couch and the bed. Both are pieces of furniture to Einstein. In the same way, a puppy will consider anything that contains him as a den, whether it is a large kennel run or crate. Einstein will come to regard your vehicle as a large crate, so why not say, "Kennel" whenever you open the door to let him enter the vehicle? When you let him out, make him wait to be released. Then allow him to exit the vehicle on the command "come."

Use your command "sit" before you give Einstein his dinner. Rather than allow him to leap around in excitement while you move to put the bowl on the floor, make him sit for a few seconds before you release him and allow him to eat. When you come home from work, make him sit before you greet him. As he comes in from outside, have him sit after he comes through the door so you can check to see if he has muddy feet. The list goes on and on.

You taught Einstein to lie by your feet while you stood on the leash. (See Chapter 13.) You can use this technique at home in various ways. Like children, most puppies want to be the center of attention when you have guests in the house and will pester them by jumping on the guests and making a thorough nuisance of themselves. The solution for many puppy owners is simply to lock up their puppies rather than address the problem. Allow Einstein to greet your guests, and then have him lie down by your chair while you put your foot on the leash. However, you need to get him used to lying in this manner before you try it when company arrives.

Sometimes an older puppy that is allowed some supervised freedom in your house will become restless during the evening when you are trying to watch one of your favorite television shows.

Rather than constantly telling Einstein to stop pestering you, insist he lie down by your chair for half an hour. Is he a nuisance in the morning when you are having that last cup of coffee before you make the beds and wash the clothes? Make him lie down next to you at the breakfast table. What do you do when you take him to the vet's office for a checkup? Many dog owners allow their dogs to visit all the other clients—human, canine, and feline. Some of these dogs are thoroughly obnoxious. The next time you take Einstein to see Dr. Doolittle, make him lie down in the office and show everyone in the waiting room how training your dog pays off. This is a good way to impress the vet as well!

Take Einstein out in the front of the house when you go to collect the mail. Have him sit, tie his leash to a solid object, and then tell him to stay. Now walk to the mailbox. Keep checking to make sure he is still sitting where you left him. If he gets up, he cannot go anywhere; however you should go right back to him and insist he stay where you left him. Place a rug on the floor in the breakfast area and make Einstein lie down and stay on the rug, rather than allowing him to beg at the table while you are eating.

Invite a friend over for coffee. Make Einstein stay in one part of the house while you go to answer the door. Tell your friend, in advance, that you are training Einstein to stay and that you may have to return to correct him more than once before you are able to answer the door. Instruct your friend to ring the doorbell intermittently until you finally let her in. The reward for her participation is a cup of coffee and a brownie!

These are just a few suggestions to test Einstein's newly acquired knowledge. Other tests may be more appropriate for your lifestyle. However, having invested this time in teaching these skills to your puppy, make sure you continue to use them throughout his lifetime since unused skills are eventually lost. A trained dog is a pleasure to own, and when you train your puppy, you present yourself to him as a leader. A dog is always happiest in the role of subordinate, so be sure to make Einstein happy by continuing to show him that you are the leader of the pack.

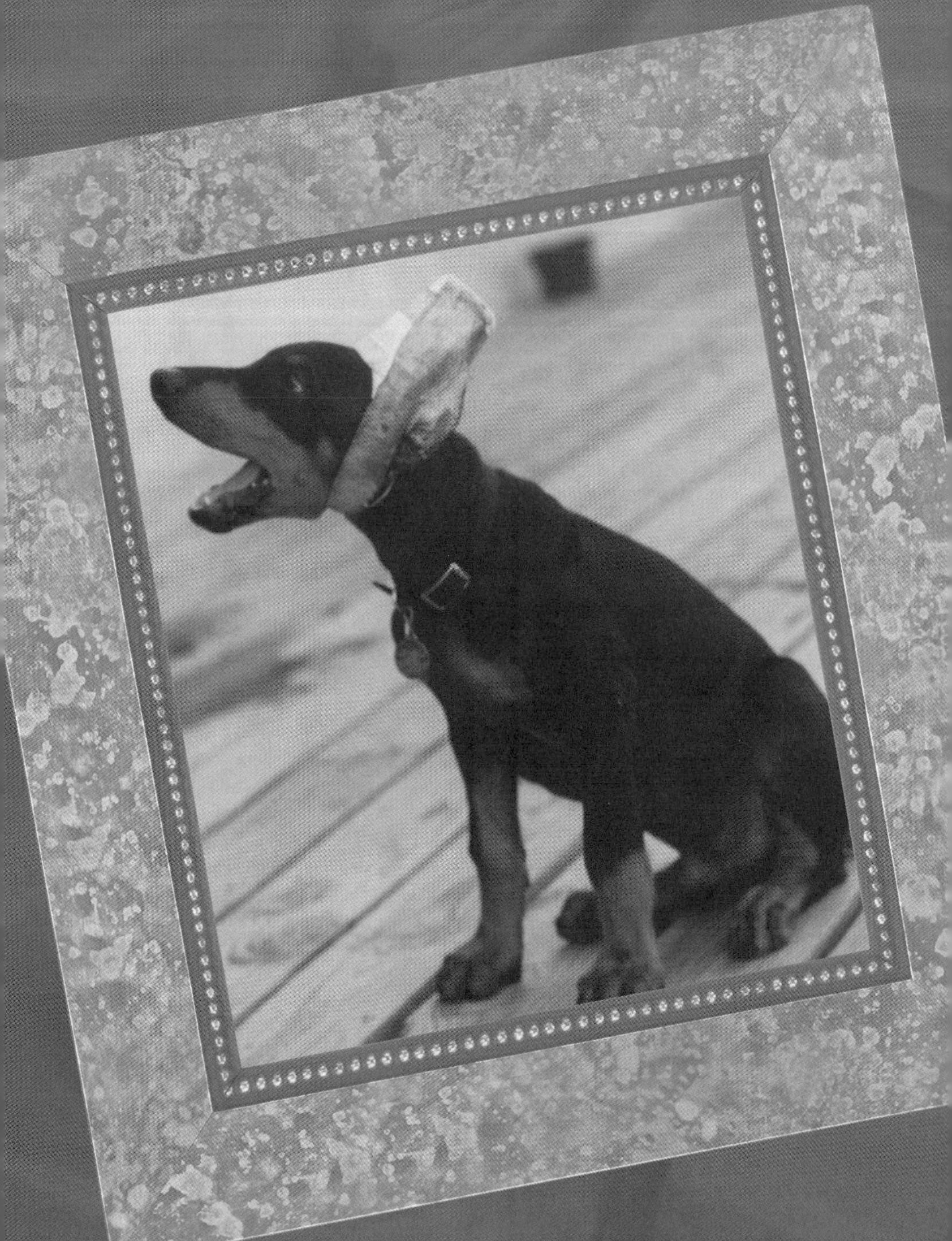

CHAPTER 15

On Being a Good Dog Neighbor

Nobody wants to fall out with a neighbor if it can possibly be avoided. Dogs, however, often cause a rift. It is not really a dog problem as much as a people problem, but of course it is the dog that gets blamed when he causes trouble.

There are three main reasons why dogs cause problems in the neighborhood. One is excessive barking. The second is elimination. The third is because of the dog running loose, turning over garbage cans, and making a general nuisance of himself. None of these three areas should present a problem for you and Einstein, if you are committed to being a good dog neighbor.

◀ There are three main reasons why dogs cause problems in the neighborhood. One is excessive barking. U-CDX, Mariah's Jeux Sont Fait UDX, sporting an ear brace, owned by Jann Cooper. *Photo by John Cooper. Doberman Pinscher, Working Group.*

BARKING ISSUES

Certain breeds of dogs are notorious barkers. A dog that barks an occasional warning is not to be faulted. It is the continuously barking dog left outside, or with access to the outside, that causes so many problems between neighbors. Some dog owners believe it is permissible to allow their dogs to bark during the day, as long as it is quiet at night. Many of these owners are away at work, and their dogs' constant barking does not annoy them. However, what about the neighbor who works the swing or night shift and is trying to sleep? What if your neighbor is retired and enjoys the luxury of lying in bed until late in the morning? There is nothing more aggravating than listening to the sound of a dog barking nonstop just outside your window.

What if you live in an apartment or condominium and own a dog that barks? Sound travels easily through walls, and a barking dog in an apartment is equally annoying as one barking out in the yard. If you and Einstein live in an apartment, or condo, be sure to check with your immediate neighbors to find out if he is barking while you are gone. If you live in a house in the suburbs and Einstein has access to the yard, then check with your neighbor to see if he is barking after you have driven off. Many dogs are quiet when the owner first leaves but then start raising a ruckus a few minutes later. Barking dogs in a rural area usually do not cause much of a problem because there are no immediate neighbors to annoy.

Barking dogs are a fact of life, but there are things a responsible dog owner can do to limit the barking. If you live in a house, must your dog have access to the outside when you are gone? A cheap and simple solution to a barking problem is to confine Einstein inside when you leave. If that is not possible, you will have to look into a means of keeping him quiet so he does not disturb the neighborhood. One solution is temporary, while the other one is permanent. Apartment dwellers have no choice. They have to do something because their dogs annoy the neighbors even when locked inside the home.

HIGH-TECH BARK COLLARS

There are collars on the market today that give a dog an electrical stimulation whenever he starts to bark. Some people consider this cruel and unusual punishment, but these types of collars are certainly effective. First, these collars do not give an electrical shock like the one you might receive if you stuck your finger into an electrical outlet. The shock is more like the static electric shock you sometimes get in the winter, as you open your car door. The stimulation is certainly unpleasant but not life threatening. Second, most of these collars can be set from a low to a high level of stimulation, so you can choose a level appropriate for your dog. The vibration of the dog's vocal cords activates these collars. Most dogs, upon receiving the stimulation from the collar, are silenced momentarily. They stop whatever they are doing, trying to figure out what just happened. When they resume barking, the same thing happens again. Dogs quickly learn to avoid the stimulation by keeping quiet.

There is another collar on the market that sprays citronella into the air instead of giving an electrical stimulation. Dogs do not like the smell of citronella and quickly learn to avoid it by being quiet. Many owners believe this type of collar is more humane. My experience has been with the other kind, but I do know people who use the citronella collar with some success.

Some dogs learn to bark right through the stimulation or actually like the smell of the citronella. If this is the case, and you are having problems with your neighbors, then you will need to look into a more permanent solution. A veterinary surgeon can remove your dog's vocal cords. Vets do this type of surgery all the time. Attend a dog show and stand near where the Shetland Sheepdogs, Collies, or Samoyeds are being shown. These breeds will be "whisper quiet" since many members have been debarked. The dogs do not know what has happened to them since they still can make noise, but the noise is so faint that, once debarked, your dog should not disturb anyone in the area where you live.

Some people want their dogs to bark to alert them that something is going on in the neighborhood. However, if your dog barks nonstop all day long, who is going to take notice if there is a prowler outside your house? If you have a dog that seldom barks and has no need of a bark collar, if your neighbor suddenly hears him barking there is a good chance he will investigate to discover the source of the commotion. People never consider how a barking dog will not attract attention if he barks constantly day in and day out. It is the dog that seldom barks who makes the best watchdog.

THE "POOP" PATROL

One area of responsibility that dog owners often shirk is to clean up after their dogs, both at home and when they take them out for a walk. If you live in a house, you should pick up his feces in the yard several times a week. If you live in an apartment or condominium, you should do this whenever you take him out to relieve himself. If you live in a hot and humid area, dog feces will begin to smell if not removed from your yard in a timely fashion. If you live in the frozen North, when the snow melts you will have a monumental task on your hands if you have not braved the elements for three months.

What does one do with dog feces? The best way to deal with the situation is twofold. If you live in a house, you can buy a bucket with a cover and place a plastic bag inside. Each day, go out in the yard, pick up the feces, and then place it in the bucket. The night before your garbage is collected, place the plastic bag out with the trash. When the weather is warm, place a paper grocery sack inside the plastic bag. For some reason, the paper sack seems to stop much of the odor that the hot weather causes. However, if you just use a paper sack instead of the plastic bag, be prepared for the sack to disintegrate from the moisture.

If you take Einstein out for a walk, take several small plastic bags with you in your pocket. Plastic grocery bags are ideal for this job. When Einstein defecates, place your hand inside one of the bags, and pick up the pile. Many dog owners find this disgusting, but you soon get used to it. Tie the bag securely, and take it home with you. Be sure to have more than one bag along. There is no guarantee that Einstein will not have to go more than once, and you do not want to be caught without a baggie. Today, many communities have ordinances that require dog owners to pick up after their dogs, and a heavy fine is imposed on those who do not. Regardless of the law, picking up after your dog makes you a good dog neighbor. If your children persuaded you to buy a dog, then you should expect them to pick up after Einstein also. It is never too early to teach them responsibility, particularly in this area.

The Stay-at-home Dog

People sometimes think it is permissible for a dog to roam the neighborhood. Dogs always roamed free in the good old days. Today, a dog's life will be short if you have this attitude. Dogs that are allowed to roam free in the countryside get shot by farmers for worrying their livestock. Dogs that roam free in suburban areas get hit by automobiles or trucks. Some dogs may be poisoned by a neighbor for constantly turning over garbage cans and creating a mess in the yard. If you do not have a fenced yard and cannot leave your dog indoors all day long, consider buying a freestanding kennel run so that your dog can remain outdoors but confined to your property.

When you bring Einstein into your home, take time to go out and introduce him to your neighbors. Open a dialog so they will know that you want to be a good neighbor. Ask them to tell you if Einstein is causing any problems. This will pay dividends in your relationship with your neighbors. Furthermore, if you are ever unaware that Einstein has gotten loose there is a good chance that one of your neighbors will bring him home or call to say he is out of your yard.

CHAPTER 16

Going Along for the Ride

Most dogs enjoy going for a ride in the car. It is never too early to start getting Einstein used to riding in a vehicle. You will need to drive him to the veterinarian, to Canine Supercuts, and to visit Grandma. However, before you put the car in gear and take Einstein for his first ride, you need to consider the following.

HERE COMES THE SUN

There is an ever-present danger lurking outside a vehicle, waiting to strike the moment you park and leave Einstein alone in the car. It is the sun! Every year a number of dogs die of heat complications when their unwitting owners leave them in the vehicle while they go into a store, into the office, or to visit a friend in her home. Even if temperatures are cool outside, if the sun is shining brightly, it only takes a few minutes for the interior of the car to

◀ Most dogs enjoy going for a ride in the car and in the boat. U-CD, Ch. Goose Creek Commentator CDX, NA, CGC, owned by "Mike" Walters-Williquette. *Photo by "Mike" Walters-Williquette. Petit Basset Griffon Vendeen, Hound Group.*

get as hot as an oven. Leaving the windows cracked an inch or two is often not sufficient to prevent the interior of the car from heating up. Some owners do take the sun into consideration when parking and wisely seek a shady spot in which to leave the vehicle. However, as the sun moves so does the shade, and before long the vehicle may be in full sun. By all means, take Einstein out for a ride on a sunny day but only if you do not have to leave him in the vehicle unattended for even a moment. It is easy to become distracted and stay away from the vehicle for longer than you intended.

Also, be aware that some dogs guard their automobiles when they believe you have left them in charge. A dog that is rushing back and forth from seat to seat, protecting your vehicle, can easily become overheated. The consequences are similar to those of parking your car in the sun.

SAFETY FIRST

How often have you seen a dog standing or moving from side to side in the back of a pickup moving at sixty miles per hour? Have you considered just how easily a dog could be thrown out should the vehicle have to brake in an emergency? Some people believe that a dog's place is riding loose in the back of a pickup. Any veterinarian will tell you of the horrendous injuries he sees each year as the result of "Trucker" deliberately or accidentally leaving the vehicle while it is moving. Some people tie their dogs in the truck bed, believing they are safer that way. A tied dog is certainly safer than a loose one. Unfortunately, if the leash is too long it still permits the dog to leave the truck and, in addition, to be dragged by the moving vehicle. If the only vehicle you own is a truck, and there is some reason why Einstein cannot ride up in the front with you, then he should ride in the back of the truck in his crate. Be sure to tie the crate securely in the truck bed. Alternatively, if you cannot use a crate, cross-tie your dog so that he cannot be thrown out. You will need to fasten a chain to either side of the truck bed so that your dog is held securely in the middle. Be sure to use a chain and not a leash since a dog can chew through a leash. Additionally, your dog will be less likely to be severely injured in an accident or sudden stop if he is secured by a harness, rather than by a collar. A dog can get whiplash as easily as a human, so it is better to attach the leashes to a harness rather than the collar around the dog's neck. Tying a dog in the back of the truck is certainly not an ideal situation, but it is better than letting him ride loose. If the only way you can travel is by having Einstein loose in the truck, then he is much better off left home.

A friend told me about an accident that happened to some people traveling through Colorado one night. They were driving a pickup truck, with their dog loosely tied in the back, when they had to brake sharply to avoid a deer. Their dog was an experienced, older dog that had ridden many a mile in the back of the truck and that had never tried to leave it of his own volition. However, when the truck braked so sharply, the owners did not notice that the dog was thrown out of the truck. It was not until they had traveled some distance down the road that they realized their dog's dilemma. The dog survived but was badly scarred from being dragged along the pavement. The owners were heartbroken over the situation. They never considered that their dog might be thrown out of the truck.

INTERIOR DELIGHT

Another reason not to leave "young Einstein" alone in the car is that the interior of the vehicle is as easily chewed as your couch cushions and kitchen cabinets. It would be simple for Einstein to reach up and pull the head lining down from the roof. I know one dog owner who had to replace the head lining of her car twice; it had been removed each time by a different puppy. Some people never seem to learn from their mistakes! Many puppies, like children, love to play at being driver when their owners leave them in the car alone. The steering wheel is about the same thickness as a Nylabone and apparently tastes similar also. One of my clients left her puppy alone in the car while she stepped into the office for a short time. When she returned, "Hoop" had almost chewed through the steering wheel. A steering wheel is a special-order item. Most automobile dealers rarely keep them in stock, and it may take several weeks to replace one.

HEADS IN

You often see dogs riding with their heads out of the window. This is a dangerous way to give your dog some fresh air. Flying debris can get into a dog's eyes, causing trauma and a trip to the vet. If you drive with your windows lowered, make sure they are only down far enough so Einstein can just poke the tip of his nose out, not his whole head.

A LITTLE AT A TIME

The first few times you take Einstein for a car ride, make it a trip around the block. I would advise you to take another person along, or even have that person drive. You cannot properly concentrate on your driving if you are trying to watch Einstein out of the corner of your eye. Many puppies get motion sickness. If this is the case with Einstein he will quickly associate a car ride with something unpleasant, so make sure the ride is over almost before it begins. When you take that first car ride, go armed with paper towels, just in case he gets sick. If Einstein does suffer from motion sickness, your veterinarian may be able to prescribe something for him to take until he outgrows the problem. Motion sickness is usually just a phase, the same as it is with children.

BUCKLE UP FOR SAFETY

For short trips around the block, Einstein can ride on your lap, as long as you are not doing the driving. When he graduates to longer trips, then it is time to consider "buckling up." The safest way to transport a dog in a vehicle is in a crate. Unfortunately, today's smaller cars make it difficult to use a crate unless you have a little dog or own a station wagon or van. If you can use a crate for transportation, do so. Make sure you secure the crate to the seat or floor so it is not tossed about if you have to brake suddenly. (See Figure 16-1.)

An acquaintance of mine became a traffic fatality some time ago. He was traveling with four dogs when the vehicle he was driving flipped over. Although it was believed he had been buckled up at the time of the accident, his seat belt was not fastened when he was

Figure 16-1. The safest way to transport a puppy in a vehicle. *Photo by Shary Singer.*

found. However, his four dogs were all riding in crates, and except for some minor cuts and bruising, they all survived the accident.

The best reason to crate a dog in the vehicle is not only for his own protection but also, in the case of an accident, the dog cannot interfere with rescue attempts by police and emergency personnel. Later, still within his crate, he can be transported to a place of safety. Should your dog be riding loose when you have an accident he may survive the impact only to be lost or injured once he is out of the vehicle. If you are traveling with Einstein, it might be a wise idea to have some particulars about him taped to a rear window of your vehicle. Should you be in an accident and become incapacitated, emergency personnel may not realize that you have a dog with you. If you have this information visible then they may look to see if your dog is nearby or at least contact a shelter to alert shelter personnel that a dog is missing in the area. The information that you post might be a current picture of Einstein, some details about his breed or mix and his size, a shot record, and a contact number at home. This is another good reason to have Einstein microchipped. Today, in this high-tech world, most shelters and veterinarians have scanners to check to see if the dog has a microchip implanted, whereby they can reunite him with his owners.

Dogs, like children, are safer riding behind the front seats. It is extremely distracting for a driver to have a dog lunging back and forth across the rear seats of the vehicle, so you should consider securing Einstein so this cannot happen. There is a simple way to do this.

Take a short piece of rope and tie a large knot at one end. Fasten a bolt snap to the other end. You will position the rope so that the knot is on the outside of the car and then close the door so that the rope is anchored securely inside. (See Figure 16-2.) Leave only enough rope inside the car so that Einstein can comfortably sit and lie down on the backseat. (See Figure 16-3.) Once you have the rope secured, then put Einstein in the back of the car, through the opposite door. Attach his collar to the snap on the rope. He really should wear a harness, but if you do not want to go to the expense of buying one then be sure he is wearing a buckle collar, not a slip collar. A dog is less likely to injure his neck in an accident if you

Figure 16-2. How to anchor the leash with the car door so that the puppy is restrained inside the vehicle. *Photo by Shary Singer.*

Figure 16-3. Leash placement inside the car, which allows the puppy enough slack to sit or lie down comfortably but is short enough that he cannot move about and distract the driver. *Photo by Shary Singer.*

restrain him by a harness instead of a collar. When Einstein gets older and used to riding in the car, you may be able to dispense with tying him in the vehicle. However, should you ever be in an accident or have to brake sharply, Einstein may take on the role of guided missile. He could be hurled right through the windshield or into the driver, causing the driver to lose control of the vehicle. If you always wear a seat belt then make sure your dog is equally restrained. Many pet supply stores sell inexpensive dog-style seat belts that attach to the regular seat belt in your car.

DON'T LEAVE HOME WITHOUT IT

Whenever you take Einstein out in the car, make sure he is wearing identification on his collar. If something should happen, and he becomes separated from you in a strange place, anyone finding him will know whom to call. Additionally, always make water available to him in the car. You can buy a non-spill travel water bowl at most pet shops.

CHAPTER 17

No Room
at the Inn

When the time comes to go on vacation, one of your concerns will probably be what to do with Einstein. Many people have an emotionally difficult time leaving their dogs behind when they take a trip. As recently as two decades ago it was relatively easy to take a vacation with your pet. Unfortunately, because of the thoughtlessness of some dog owners, many motels no longer put out the welcome mat for Man's Best Friend. People on vacation have left their dogs alone in motel rooms for hours at a time while they enjoyed the facilities of the resort. Their dogs, afraid that they had been abandoned, barked the entire time their owners were out of the room, thus disturbing other guests. In addition, canine guests have torn up the furnishings in the room or eliminated on the car-

◀ There are very few beaches left in the United States where dogs can enjoy the surf and the sand. *Photo by "Mike" Walters-Williquette. Cardigan Welsh Corgi, Herding Group (left); Petit Basset Griffon Vendeen, Hound Group (right).*

pet or bedspread. Through no fault of yours, you may find there is "no room at the inn" when you try to check in with Einstein.

Touring with Einstein

If you do decide to take Einstein on vacation with you, then planning ahead is advisable. Make inquiries in advance to be sure your dog is welcome wherever you plan to spend the night. Do not be surprised if the motel adds a special room-cleaning charge to your bill. It takes additional time for the housekeeping staff to remove pet hair from the carpet. One popular motel chain limits the size of the canine guest to twenty-five pounds. Many motels today require that you take your dog with you whenever you leave the room. This can present a problem if it is hot outside. What will you do with Einstein when it is 90° and you cannot leave him in an air-conditioned room while you go out for dinner? You may end up calling room service.

There is a book that has been on the market for years called *Touring with Towzer,* which that lists dog-friendly motels, hotels, and bed-and-breakfast establishments. You might wish to obtain a copy if you plan to vacation with Einstein.

Camping with a Canine

Dogs are usually welcome at many RV parks throughout the United States. Some parks only allow dogs if the guest is traveling in a motor home, fifth wheel, or travel trailer. Park management has learned the hard way that a dog can easily chew its way out of a tent and then go on a rampage throughout the park. If you go camping, be sure to check with the RV park to make sure Einstein can accompany you. Tenting with a dog can be dangerous if you are staying in an area where bears may be on the prowl.

Vacation Spots

There are few beaches left in the United States where dogs can enjoy the surf and the sand. National parks do not permit dogs beyond the boundaries of parking lots. Theme parks, like Disney World, have kennels available for the pets of guests. Today, there are few places where you can vacation with Einstein, so perhaps he would be better off left at home. Remember that absence makes the heart grow fonder.

STAYING IN OTHER PEOPLE'S HOMES

When you go on vacation, do you plan to visit relatives or friends? Not everyone will be as enamoured with Einstein as you are. If you visit family or friends, be sure to check to make certain your dog is as welcome as you are. If there is a resident dog or cat, that animal may not take kindly to a visiting canine cousin. Many a friendship has been ruined when the guest's dog and the resident dog or cat have an altercation. It is particularly upsetting if one of the animals gets injured. Furthermore, a visiting dog occasionally destroys something of value in the home where he is a guest, causing a rift in the relationship between friends or relatives. If Einstein receives an invitation to go with you on vacation, be sure to take his crate along so that he cannot destroy anything if you leave him alone in a strange house.

LEAVING EINSTEIN BEHIND

For simplicity's sake, you may find it wiser to leave Einstein behind when you travel. Your next course of action is to make a decision as to who will take care of Einstein. Before you make that final determination, consider the choices available to you.

A NEIGHBOR

If you have a fenced backyard so that Einstein does not have to be walked off the property, you might be able to use the services of a reliable neighbor. However, a young dog left home alone will definitely get into trouble. Using a neighbor as caretaker may be a possibility with an older dog, but I would not recommend it with a puppy.

A FRIEND

Friends sometimes offer to look after your dog, but friends are usually not equipped to do so as safely as a pet care professional. If something should happen to Einstein while you are off enjoying your vacation, would your friendship survive? A former client once left her dog with a friend while vacationing. All went well until Sunday morning when the paperboy left the gate that led to the street open. When the dog was let out in what was supposed to be a secure backyard, there was a sudden screech of brakes, a thud, and later the loss of a friendship. This situation can be even worse should it happen when you leave Einstein with a relative. It is often impossible to end a relationship with a relative, but continued contact may be painful for both of you.

A PET SITTING SERVICE

Many dog owners avail themselves of a pet sitting service. Again, if your dog is older this may be the answer, but not with a young puppy. If the sitter lets your dog out only twice a day, he may start soiling the house—that is, unless he has access to the outside through a doggie door. Many pet sitters make last rounds at 7 P.M., and do not reappear for the next visit before 8 A.M. the following morning. Confining your dog to the house for thirteen hours at a stretch is asking for trouble. Some dogs will not allow pet sitters access to the house when they arrive to let them out. If you are considering the services of a pet sitter, you should do a trial run. Prior to your vacation, ask the sitter to come and let out Einstein while you sit in your car parked a few houses down the street. If the pet sitter runs into Ivan the Terrible, instead of Einstein your friend, you will still have time to make other arrangements for his care.

A VETERINARIAN

Leaving your dog with a veterinarian has its good and bad points. Remember that many dogs visiting a veterinary hospital are sick, and you do not want to expose Einstein to sick dogs unnecessarily. If the kennel building is separate from the hospital then this should not be a problem. If you have a dog that is likely to fret, which in turn may make your dog ill, then boarding your dog where a vet is in attendance may be an excellent idea. If your dog has health problems like epilepsy, then supervision by a veterinarian is recommended.

A Boarding Kennel

Boarding a dog at a kennel is probably the most practical solution. Most kennels are secure so that, should your dog get loose, he cannot leave the facility. Check out the security of the kennel when you make your inspection. There should be a fence to prevent any dog from reaching the street. Many kennel owners live on site and are therefore able to monitor the dogs more closely than is possible with a house sitter. Some dog owners consider a kennel to be a last resort when it comes to leaving their dogs behind. This is unfortunate. Many kennels are well run, and the proprietors are devoted to their canine guests. Most kennel owners are proud of their establishments and happy to show a potential human client the facilities where the client's dog will spend his time.

Check Things Out Ahead of Time

Ask dog-owning friends for kennel recommendations. Additionally, before you make arrangements to leave Einstein at a kennel, call ahead and ask for a tour. Be aware that there are busy times at a kennel, like Spring Break and Christmas. If you ask to see the facilities at one of these times, your request is not likely to be greeted with enthusiasm. Inquire as to a good time to view the kennel so that the owner will have time to spend with you and answer your concerns regarding Einstein's stay. How can you tell if a kennel is good or bad? A bad sign is feces lying in empty runs. Excessive barking coming from the kennel, before you disturb the dogs by your visit, is not a good sign either. If you are hit by a strong odor of urine and feces when the kennel door is opened, you may want to check out a different facility. Dogs in a kennel should appear happy, and as you are given the grand tour, you should notice the help addressing the dogs by name. Any bedding for the dogs to lie on should appear clean. There should be no food spilled on the floor, unless you happen to arrive to inspect the facilities during feeding time. Some dogs, in their excitement to eat, knock food from the bowl. Water in bowls or buckets should be clean, and the containers should have water in them.

Do not make unrealistic demands for Einstein's stay. Dog owners often want to bring their dogs' own food and ask for a price break for doing so. Do not be surprised to learn that you will be assessed an extra charge if the kennel is required to feed your dog food that you provide. Feeding dogs at a kennel is on a par with an assembly line. It takes additional time to stop and dish up individual diets. Some owners like to leave special bedding for their pets and then become angry if the bedding gets destroyed. Favorite toys often get lost or stolen by another canine guest. Do not ask for special privileges for Einstein. Kennel owners have good reasons why they only allow certain objects to be left in the runs with their guests.

Some kennels offer an exercise program, or fitness program as it is often known. This entails a dog getting supervised activity outside the individual kennel run. Most kennels have an additional charge for this service, but it is well received by both owner and dog. Many owners are happier knowing Sport is getting a chance to stretch his legs every day.

Be sure to abide by the kennel's opening hours policy. Although the owners may live on the premises, they will have certain hours to drop off and pick up your dog. It is unsettling to the entire kennel if someone arrives late to get her pet and all the dogs have already been put to bed for the night. Should you do this, do not be surprised to pay an extra fee for late checkout, just as you would do at a regular motel. You will likely have to pay additional charges if Einstein has to be medicated. Consider having Einstein bathed before you take him home. No matter how clean a kennel is kept, your dog will still not smell as good as he did when you dropped him off. Some kennels give a courtesy bath for a dog boarded for a certain number of days.

STARTING EARLY

When Einstein is a puppy, you should introduce him to kennel life early on. A younger dog is much more adaptable than an older dog when it comes to being left in a strange place. You may have every intention of always hiring a house sitter, until the day you find your sitter unavailable. We once got a call to board a nineteen-year-old Dachshund. This dog had never been left in a kennel; a sitter had always come to the house to look after him. There was a death in the family, and the Dachsie's owners had no choice but to leave town immediately. For the first time, their sitter was not available, so a friend recommended us. We were apprehensive about boarding such an ancient dog, one that had never had any kennel experience. However, Fritz did just fine. We never expected to see Fritz again, but only a month later he returned. Unbelievably, there was another death in the family. However, this time the owners chose to leave him with us rather than a house sitter because they knew we were always around to see to the comfort of their old pet. Fortunately for us, boarding Fritz turned out well, but that might not always be the case with a dog that is not used to staying in a kennel. You would be well advised to expose Einstein to kennel life for a couple of days even if you are not going on vacation. You want him to discover that going to "camp" is not a bad thing. Many dogs enjoy the companionship of the other dogs staying at the kennel and literally drag their owners through the entrance to "camp." They cannot get there soon enough.

CHAPTER 18

The Patter of Tiny Paws

Pet owners decide to breed their dogs for three main reasons. The first is for financial gain. The second is because they want another dog just like the one they have. The final reason is to show their children the miracle of birth. If you have not made the commitment to have Einstein neutered, or Ms. Einstein spayed, you need to take a hard look at why breeding is not such a good idea.

FINANCIAL GAIN

If you bought Einstein from a breeder, you just might consider trying to recoup your money or decide to begin breeding dogs for a second income. People believe they can make money by breeding dogs. They remember how much they spent to buy theirs. They

◀ Many pet owners never contemplate the time, money, and commitment required to breed a litter of puppies. *Photo by Ann Ramsey. Pembroke Welsh Corgis, Herding Group.*

forget to consider how much it costs to do it right. If you bought Einstein from a reputable breeder, the breeder probably gave you copies of certificates that showed the hip and eye evaluations of Einstein's parents. The Orthopedic Foundation for Animals (OFA) or Penn-Hip certifies a dog to be free of hip dysplasia, a crippling disease of the hips. Hip dysplasia is hereditary, so if your dog has this disease you must never breed him. The Canine Eye Registration Foundation (CERF) certifies that a dog is free of hereditary eye diseases, many of which cause blindness. In addition, some breeds have a problem with a poorly functioning thyroid or a blood-clotting disorder. There are many different hereditary diseases affecting dogs, and nobody should breed a dog without first determining the dog is free of genetic defects. Should you decide to breed Einstein, consult your veterinarian first so he can advise you as to which genetic tests need to be performed. These tests and certifications cost money. An X ray for OFA certification is likely to cost around $100. The certification done by the OFA itself is an additional $25, even more if your breed needs elbow certification as well. A CERF examination has to be performed by a board-certified veterinary ophthalmologist, and there are few veterinarians with these credentials. Many breeders have to drive several hundred miles to attend a clinic where a veterinary ophthalmologist is practicing. Travel expenses quickly add to the cost of raising a litter of puppies.

Before you sell a puppy, you must have it checked by your veterinarian to make sure that it is healthy and to get its first inoculations. All of this takes a large chunk of change out of your plans to make a small fortune as a dog breeder. Now, what happens if you cannot sell the puppies? You should not breed a dog unless you have homes for every puppy expected. How many people can say that they do? Not many!

What do you do if you have problems with the bitch or the puppies? This can bankrupt you in a hurry. Many bitches end up having to have a cesarean section. Murphy's Law usually steps in at this point! Many bitches give birth (whelp) in the middle of the night or on the weekend. If your dog runs into difficulty, you will face an emergency visit to your animal hospital. Emergency calls are far more expensive than a regular office visit. Sometimes your veterinarian is not available, and you will have to deal with a different doctor. This can be unsettling for the owner in a time of stress. Puppies born by cesarean section often do not survive. Not only will you have to pay for an expensive operation—you may have few or no puppies to sell to pay for the surgery. After a cesarean section, the mother is sometimes unable to care for the litter. Guess on whose hands this falls?

I am sure you love Ms. Einstein. A few years ago, a neighbor of mine decided to breed her bitch. This bitch had an outstanding personality and had passed hip and eye evaluations. Every potential puppy in the litter had a home eagerly awaiting its arrival. Unfortunately, when it came time for the whelping there was a problem. My neighbor was inexperienced at breeding dogs and waited too long to contact the vet when the puppies failed to arrive on time. When she finally realized there was a problem, she rushed Freckles to the animal hospital, where the veterinarian performed a cesarean section. Freckles had eight puppies, but by the time the veterinarian performed the cesarean section it was too late. The dead puppies, left too long in the womb, caused Freckles to become toxic, and she died shortly after the surgery. My neighbor was devastated, as we all were. She had never envisioned this situation when she decided Freckles should have a litter of puppies.

Even if your bitch does not need a cesarean section, she still may be unable to care for her puppies. If this is the case, they will have to be bottle-fed around the clock. This will mean very little sleep for you since a puppy needs feeding every two hours at first. Can you afford to take time off work to stay home with a litter of puppies, if necessary? Once weaned, puppies eat a lot of food. This is another way they put a dent in your profits.

If you do not have homes for all your puppies, you will have to advertise in order to sell them. This costs money. However, this may be the only way to find homes for all of them. In the past, some of your friends or neighbors may have casually mentioned how much they like Ms. Einstein. They may have told you that if you ever bred her they would consider taking one of the puppies.

Of course, when the time comes they may have a million excuses why they cannot take one. Are you prepared to keep the puppies for several extra weeks, until you can find suitable homes for them? What will you do if there are no homes available? This is one reason why shelters are overflowing with unwanted dogs. People do not think things through.

YOU WANT A SECOND EINSTEIN

Those of us who compete in performance events with our dogs would like to reproduce the dogs we show. When you breed your dog, there is no guarantee that the puppies will turn out to be just like him. Genetics are unpredictable. In fact, you have a better chance of getting a dog similar to yours by going back to your dog's parents! Only the most outstanding dogs should be reproduced, and then this should be left to the experts.

YOU WANT TO TEACH YOUR CHILDREN THE MIRACLE OF BIRTH

This is fine, as long as you first introduce your children to the real world. The real world has an overpopulation of dogs and cats. Children need to learn what happens to these unfortunate animals when there is no home available. Before you breed Einstein, take your children to the shelter to meet these unwanted pets. Remain there and show them what happens to these animals when their time for adoption passes by. If you do not think this is an appropriate topic for your children, then reconsider having them experience the miracle of birth. However, if you are still considering adding another dog to the family, you can teach your children a valuable lesson. Instead of breeding Einstein, explain the reason why you cannot do this; then adopt one of the dogs you meet at the shelter.

Many pet owners never contemplate the time, money, and commitment required to breed a litter. If they really thought about it, they probably would never consider doing so. Now that you understand all the problems with canine overpopulation, take responsibility and neuter your pet. This surgery can be done as young as four months of age. Do not let Einstein add to the statistics at the shelter. No matter how careful you are, if your bitch is in heat there is always the possibility that she may get out and become pregnant. If Einstein is an intact male, then remember what happened to my friend's dog, Romeo. Before she had time to get Romeo neutered, he went looking for love and unfortunately was hit by a car. Romeo did not have a chance. Think about Einstein's future and get him neutered before it is too late.

If Einstein is a "pound puppy" then you probably have a contract with the shelter to get Einstein neutered or spayed. In fact, many shelters require a dog or cat to be neutered before it is released for adoption.

Humane Society
South Branch
Please Help Us
Mon.– Fri. 10-5 Sat. 10-3 closed Sunday

Taking Over Someone Else's Problem

Adopting a puppy from a shelter is a little different than acquiring a puppy from a breeder. You should consider a puppy abandoned at a shelter as a special needs puppy. It is unlikely that the puppy received the handling and socialization that is so important to its mental development. People who allow their dogs to breed indiscriminately are unlikely to take good care of a litter when it is born. This is particularly true of the litter that ends up at a shelter. People often "dump" a litter as soon as the puppies can walk, at about four weeks of age, although they are prepared to tell the staff at the shelter that the puppies are seven weeks old. People like this do not want to spend any money on puppy food and shots, nor

◄ Adopting a puppy from a shelter is a little different than acquiring a puppy from a breeder. *Photo by Margret Taylor. Mixed-breed.*

take responsibility for the litter. If you should adopt a puppy from a shelter, you may have difficulty training him in the beginning because he could be considerably younger than you have been led to believe. A puppy less than seven weeks of age is hard to train to do anything. Therefore, if you are having difficulty, it might be because your puppy is too young to learn much. If training improves in a couple of weeks then you can take a guess that Einstein was only five weeks old when the shelter was told he was eight.

Owners of shelter puppies have often told me that, because their puppies cringe when anyone tries to touch them, they must have been abused before they found their way to the shelter. A more likely scenario is that the puppies are shy because they had little or no human contact during the critical age of three to seven weeks. It is during those few short weeks that the bond is formed between puppies and humans. Therefore, if your puppy acts afraid of you or other people, you will have to spend extra time socializing him so that he becomes less afraid of human contact.

If you happen to adopt an older puppy from the shelter, one that is three months of age or older, you may be taking over someone else's problem. People do not usually choose to take good dogs to shelters except because of serious, immediate problems in their own lives. The more likely scenario is that the owners grew tired of a dog with which they were having problems. However, potentially good dogs end up in shelters all the time. Dogs left at a shelter most likely have not received the training necessary to turn them into good pets. Once someone takes time to train them, then they should become the good dogs that rarely find their way into a shelter. The potential is there, but it needs to be brought out.

With this thought in mind, you may have to treat this older puppy just as you would one that is seven weeks of age. Because most people recycle a dog due to house soiling, chewing, and biting problems, you may face dealing with one, two, or all three of these problems at once. Read Chapter 9, "Teaching Your Puppy the Right Way to Live," and then put the suggestions into practice with your recycled puppy. A puppy that already has some bad habits is going to take longer to train. It is always more difficult to redo anything than to do it right the first time. However, an older puppy has a longer attention span, which is an asset in training.

If you adopt an adult dog from a shelter, then follow the previously suggested guidelines. Until the dog shows you otherwise, consider he will probably soil the house and chew on the furniture. The dog profile given out at the shelter is usually based on what the previous owners told the staff when they left the dog at the shelter. There is no way for the staff members to know, for certain, if the dog is actually housebroken. They can only go on what the owners told them. They will not know if he chews destructively since he will be housed in an area where there are no chairs and couch cushions on which to chew. They will not know if the dog is good with children. It is unlikely that children would be allowed to spend time alone with a dog in a run. The shelter would face a major lawsuit should one of the dogs attack a child on the premises. Even if the shelter does allow canine/child interaction, it would most likely be under the supervision of an adult. If this is the case, you still might not get a true picture as to whether the dog is completely trustworthy around children. Therefore, if an older dog at the shelter appeals to you, adopt it for itself, not for the training you were told the puppy had received. If you do, you are likely to be disappointed once you get him home.

Sometimes the dog that appeals to you arrived at the shelter as a stray. Occasionally, a good dog ends up becoming lost. His owners may be frantically searching for him, but the dog may have wandered too far away, and they may be unable to locate him. If this is the case, you may end up with an exceptionally well-trained dog without having to do any training yourself.

Some people are reluctant to adopt an older dog from a shelter and instead look in the classified section of the local paper for an older puppy. It is worth noting that an older puppy advertised in the paper is just as likely to have similar behavior problems as one that you would find at a shelter. In the case of a puppy advertised in the paper, his owner may be concerned about what is going to happen to his puppy more than the owner who takes his puppy to the shelter. This owner is attempting to find his puppy a new home, rather than leaving it to chance that someone will adopt the dog at the shelter. Unfortunately, many shelters are forced by overcrowding to dispose of any dogs and cats that are still living in the shelter after a few days internment.

Older puppies that find their way into the classified section of the paper are just like dogs that end up at the shelter. They are potentially good dogs that may have a few problems. However, the owner will rarely tell you the true reason why she can no longer house the puppy. You will hear excuses like, "My child is allergic to him," which may mean that the dog is biting the child. She may tell you that the puppy is "an outside dog that needs room to run." This usually means the puppy is destroying the house and will not come when called. When you are told a four-month-old puppy is "house-trained," then the owner is being economical with the truth, or perhaps she has not noticed he is urinating in the house.

As with adopting a shelter puppy, if you acquire an older puppy through an advertisement in the classifieds, when you bring him home you should start his training from scratch. Do not allow him to have the run of the house, only to discover he is not housebroken. Instead, confine him just as you would if he were seven weeks old. When you leave the house, confine him to a crate or to an ex-pen. Do not believe the owner who tells you that the puppy is not destructive. Would you really have taken him home if you knew he would eliminate in the house and destroy your valuable possessions?

If you have a particular breed in mind, then you might consider purebred rescue. Many national and local breed clubs have older dogs of their breed that for various reasons need to find new homes. Someone familiar with the breed usually evaluates the dogs that enter breed rescue. These people make sure that there are no health or temperament problems that need attention before the dog is put up for adoption. Until the right home is found, these dogs live in the home of a rescuer and are given some basic training if needed. You can obtain information on purebred rescue by contacting the parent club of the breed you would like to own. In addition, some shelters list the contact names of breed rescue in the area. Many national breed clubs have Web sites on the Internet. You can usually get a link to these sites by visiting the home page of the AKC.

Many dog behavior problems are solvable, but they will take time and effort on your part. When you adopt a dog from the shelter or from purebred rescue, you are probably saving a life. If you follow the guidelines on training, you can turn the dog around and give him something that some other human took away from him—the chance to be a good dog and a wonderful companion.

CHAPTER 20

When Good
Dogs Go Bad

It will seem like no time at all before Einstein grows from little puppy to adult dog. While most puppies are born with nice temperaments, a few are born with nasty dispositions. If Einstein happens to be one of the minority, it would have been obvious almost from the start of your relationship. Some puppies begin their lives as nice dogs but then for some reason change as they reach maturity or change even as mature adult dogs. Therefore, if Einstein has always been easy to get along with and his personality suddenly starts to change, you must consider that something physical might be the cause and consult your veterinarian.

If Einstein is a male and not neutered, hormones could play a part in this change. During puberty, young adult dogs may display dominance, aggression, and territorialism. If this is the case with

◀ Allergies and skin problems can cause a dog to become irritable. Bearfoot, owned by Lisa Kuhn. *Photo by Nelson Enochs. Chinese Shar-pei, Non-sporting Group.*

Einstein, then by having him neutered he should return to being the dog you owned before puberty changed his personality.

If you have ruled out hormones as a reason for Einstein's personality change, then there are other possibilities to consider as to why he is not as easy to get along with as he once was. If he is growling or snapping when he is lying down and you attempt to pet him, could he be in pain? You know yourself that if you are sick or hurting your disposition may not be at its best. Young dogs are normally quite active and play hard. A variety of orthopedic problems can occur that may cause your puppy's behavior to change. Most of them range from causing minor discomfort to causing acute pain. The more common problems are osteochondrosis, elbow dysplasia, patella luxation, and hip dysplasia. With the exception of patella luxation, these problems are more commonly found in larger dogs. Back problems are also quite common in certain breeds. If you have ever suffered from back pain, you know how miserable it makes you feel. If your dog is not acting himself, nor running around like he once did, he could be having discomfort. A trip to the vet for a physical might be the order of the day.

Loss of vision and hearing can also cause a change in personality. If your dog does not see or hear your approach, he may become startled and react by snapping or spooking. Other eye problems can cause pain, like entropion (eyelashes that turn in and rub on the eyeball) and glaucoma.

Allergies and skin problems can also cause a dog to become irritable. The skin covers the entire body, wraps around the toes, and lines the ears. Irritation of the skin may result in self-mutilation, licking, and scratching. Dogs with allergies often have difficulty functioning normally because they are so busy scratching and chewing on themselves. To relieve the itching, the vet may place a dog on a cortisone-type drug. This usually causes a dog to drink excessive amounts of water, which in turn creates the need to urinate more frequently. Bitches sometimes get bladder infections, which often cause incontinence. Bladder and kidney stones are common problems in some breeds and can cause a dog to eliminate a lot more frequently. If any of these conditions occur, an otherwise clean dog may begin urinating in the house if he has no means of getting outside while you are away from home. Sometimes an owner does not realize what is happening and believes her dog is soiling the house deliberately when in fact he is ill.

Metabolic disorders can change a dog's personality. Many breeds suffer from thyroid problems, which cause weight gain and lethargy. Once diagnosed and treated, your dog should go back to being his normal self. Cardiac and respiratory problems can occur in puppies and slowly worsen as the puppy grows into adulthood. A puppy that sleeps a lot and tires easily may have a medical problem.

Finally, some dogs become mentally ill, just like humans. There is even doggie Prozac on the market to treat abnormal behavior. For some reason, people never seem to consider that a dog can have a mental illness, such as a personality disorder; they just think their dogs are being willful.

If your dog starts behaving in an abnormal manner, do not simply put it down to misbehavior nor to a stage in your dog's life. Most dogs' personalities do not change radically between puppy and adulthood. Consult your veterinarian. Then, if you rule out a health issue, contact a dog-behavior specialist to come up with an answer to Einstein's problem.

CHAPTER 21

A Trip down Memory Lane

When you have made a career out of dogs, as I have, there are usually some incidents that stand out in your mind as worth sharing with others. In addition, there is usually a moral to most of these stories. When my husband Dick and I first met, we both owned Golden Retrievers, and in addition, I had two longhaired Dachshunds. Many of these stories involve the Goldens we owned rather than our current Border Collies. You might think that this is because the Border Collies are so smart that they do not get into difficulties. The fact of the matter is that we have become much smarter in our dealings with our dogs. Through experience, we no longer place our dogs in certain situations where they might be at risk.

When I was a teenager growing up in England, I used to drive an "old banger," the name the British give to an old car. I was very proud of my 1932 Morris Minor two-seater convertible, and

◄ Taking photographs of your puppy, particularly during the holidays, is one way you can look back down Memory Lane. *Photo by Kohler Photography. Boxers, Working Group.*

unless it was pouring rain, I always drove with the top down no matter the weather. One Saturday, on a crisp winter morning, I was driving along the main shopping street of Loughton, a bustling suburb east of London. My passenger that day was our family Miniature Poodle, Sam, who was riding next to me on the front seat. As is typical of old bangers, my car chose that moment to break down, right in the middle of the High Street, causing a minor traffic jam. The local constable, who was walking the beat on the other side of the road, crossed over to assist me. "Here young lady, let me give you a hand," he said. "Let's get your old banger off the street. Out you get and help to push, and I'll steer." Without giving Sammy a second thought I jumped out of the car and went to lean against the spare tire while the bobby reached into the car to grip the steering wheel. Sam, who for some reason hated anyone in uniform, promptly bit the constable as he put his hand on the wheel. Fortunately, because it was a bitterly cold day, the bobby was wearing heavy leather gloves, and Sam barely broke the skin. The bobby was nice about it and said he should have known better than to reach into a car with a dog sitting on the seat. "OK, miss," he then said. "You steer, and I'll push." We got the car off the road, and the policeman went back to his beat. And Sam? Well, nothing happened. England is rabies-free, so there is no quarantine for dog bites. If this had been the United States, it is doubtful that the outcome would have been quite the same.

Moral: Never reach in a car when there is a dog inside. You never know how protective the dog may be.

Before I began a career in dogs, my passion was waterskiing. Almost every weekend of the summer was spent at the lake with friends who owned a ski boat. They owned two toy breeds, while I had two Dachshunds, and all four dogs went out with us in the boat. One of their toys, a Pomeranian, was a menace in the boat when anyone tried to go skiing. Every time someone jumped in the water, Squeaky would rush forward and try to bite the skier on the legs as she went over the side. One day, either Squeaky was faster than usual or I was too slow, and he made contact with my ankle as I started to jump into the water. I saw red, quite literally, and the moment I surfaced, I reached up to where Squeaky was peering gleefully over the side and hauled him down into the lake. Squeaky never liked to get wet and never went near the lake when he was on dry land, so I held him in the water for several minutes. My reaction at the time was instinctive and based on anger, not on the knowledge I have acquired today. Squeaky really hurt me when he bit my ankle, and I was seeing red. Later, after I cooled down and my ankle was not quite so painful, I handed Squeaky back to someone in the boat and started skiing. Squeaky disappeared under a seat in the boat and remained there until we reached the shore. The next day when we went out, I was ready for him, but guess what—the moment I went and stood in the back of the boat, Squeaky dove under the seat and did not reappear until I was in the water. From that moment on, any time anyone stood in the back of the boat ready to go skiing, Squeaky hid. His owners were happy with the outcome because, while they did not condone his behavior, they had no idea how to stop it.

Moral: Timing is everything.

Many years ago, before the scientific community eventually recognized the benefits of pets visiting patients in hospitals, I learned firsthand about the remarkable effects of the human-animal bond. One of my students and her son were injured in a terrible explosion, while the family dog escaped unharmed. I ended up keeping the dog because my student and her son remained in the hospital for many months and there was nobody else to take care of the dog. The boy was badly injured, and he was hanging between life and death. Through it all, he kept asking about his dog, sensing that perhaps his pet might have been killed in the explosion.

The dog was a smaller breed that could easily be smuggled into the hospital if the opportunity presented itself. The hospital was several hundred miles away, so a friend and I drove eight hours to visit them, taking the dog along in the hope that we could sneak him into the hospital to see his owners. When we arrived to visit our friends, the boy's personal nurse told us that everyone knew just how much the dog meant to the boy but regulations had to be followed. The dog could not be allowed in the hospital. She also mentioned, in passing, that she would not be around to check on her patient for the next hour and, following that, the doctor would be making his rounds. As she left the room she told us that the easiest way to reach the parking lot, if we needed to go down there for any reason, was via the service elevator only a couple of doors from the room. As she went out of the door, she winked.

We rushed down to the car and carried the dog, hidden under a couple of jackets, into the elevator and up to the boy's room. There was a very emotional reunion between the boy, his dog, and my student. Some time later, the nurse came down the hall and, without putting her head around the door, reminded us that the doctor's rounds would be in ten minutes. We quickly ran for the service elevator and returned the dog to the car. We later learned that the doctor in charge said that on that very day the boy regained the will to live and the doctor wondered what had caused such a sudden change. Of course, everyone on the staff guessed the reason why. Happily, the boy recovered from his terrible injuries, but I wonder what the outcome might have been had his nurse not been so understanding.

Before we owned our boarding facility, we used to keep dogs in the basement of the house we were renting. We exercised the dogs in a fenced-in area on one side of the house. One day, I got a call from a lady who wanted to board her year old Chihuahua for two weeks while she went on vacation with her children. I should have been suspicious when she dropped the dog off and told me if I had any problems to call her husband at home, since he was not going with them. She mentioned that he did not like the dog and refused to look after him while she was away. I quickly learned the reason why. When I went to let out Samson, which was in fact his name, he wanted no part of me touching him. I could not get anywhere near him for two days. I eventually managed to get a leash on his collar, and I used it to take him upstairs to relieve himself in an exercise pen within the fence.

One day while I was taking Samson out of the pen to bring him back inside the house, he managed to slip out of his collar and started running loose within the fenced yard. There was a large space under the gate, and I was concerned that, small as he was, he could escape if he headed in that direction. I tried to herd him back in the pen and down into the basement, but I could get nowhere near him. I called for Dick to come to help me, but he was on the other side of the house and could not hear my calls. I could not leave Samson while I went to get a towel that I could throw over him so I could grab him without getting bitten, in case he went under the gate. Therefore, my only recourse was to remove the shirt I was wearing and use it in place of a towel.

At the time, we were living in the country, and our house was relatively isolated. We shared a driveway with our neighbor, Tom, who was away at work. As I was racing around the yard in just my bra and jeans, low and behold Tom came driving up the driveway. He sat in his car and watched in amusement as I tried unsuccessfully to catch a "greased pig." He eventually came to my assistance, and Samson was duly cornered and caught. From that day forward, Samson was never allowed out of the basement, and we never boarded Samson again.

Moral: Always be suspicious of a dog that one of the family members will not look after.

Shortly after Dick and I got together, we made an offer on a very old house that needed extensive renovations. At that point in our lives, we were financially strapped and had to count every cent. Because our offer had been accepted, we decided to celebrate and, on our way home from training our dogs, stopped at the grocery store and treated ourselves to steak, a bottle of wine, and some items from the deli counter. In addition, we bought some other staples and a box of semi-moist dog food for a dog we were boarding at the time.

Rather than going directly home, we drove by the new house to see what work needed doing in the yard, and while we were there we met our neighbors for the first time. Loose in the wagon were our two obedience champions, Harvey (a Golden Retriever) and Gretl (a longhaired Dachshund). We were away from the vehicle for longer than we planned while first we visited with the neighbors and then walked about the yard. On our return to the wagon I found my Dachshund sitting meekly on the front seat, while to our horror we discovered that our dinner, the Hawaiian salad, the roast turkey, and much of the dog food was missing. All that remained of the steaks was the Styrofoam tray and plastic wrap in which they had been displayed. Even the box of semi-moist dog food was open, and a number of packages were missing.

When I saw what had happened, I burst into tears. Dick tried to comfort me to no avail. He finally produced some money that he had hidden away in his wallet and told me to dry my eyes because we would go and buy another steak. Through my tears I told him that I was not crying because our food was gone but because I knew his dog, Harvey, had eaten everything while my poor little Gretl got none. To this day, we still laugh over the incident and the reason I was crying.

Moral: No matter how well-trained you think your dog is, never leave him alone in the car with the groceries.

One hot July day, on our way home from a dog show, we stopped to swim our dogs at a deserted lake where there was a public swimming beach. At the time, we were the only people there. Traveling with us in our wagon was one of our students, who also owned a Golden, but her dog was not an experienced swimmer, as ours were. We began throwing retrieving dummies for the dogs, and all was going smoothly until our student's dog tried instead to retrieve one of the plastic buoys that marked off the designated swimming area from the rest of the lake. At first, we did not realize what was happening when the dog did not return with the others. On further scrutiny, it became clear that her dog was trapped by the rope running between the buoys. Dick said to our student, "Hey, you'd better go in and get him before he drowns." My student said, "I can't. I don't have a swimsuit with me. Can't you go and get him?" Dick replied, "Hey, it's your stupid dog. I guess you are going to have to strip."

After a few moments hesitation, in which she was hoping that Dick would take pity on her and go to rescue her dog himself, she did just that. She stripped right down to her tiny lace panties and bra while my husband looked on in amusement. It took her several minutes to swim out to her dog and release him, and just as she was walking out of the water and onto the beach, two carloads of people arrived at the lake. Our student looked for somewhere to hide, but there was nothing around but beach. Fortunately, since she had dry clothes lying on the beach, she was able to look reasonably presentable on her way home.

Moral: If you take your dog swimming, always wear a swimsuit, just in case.

Later that summer we spent a week with some friends in a cabin by a lake. On the shore near the cabin was the nest of a mother duck with nine ducklings. My well-trained Golden obedience champion, Pippa, discovered the nest that first afternoon and immediately swam after the duck and her brood, ignoring my calls to return to shore. To direct my dog's attention away from her babies, the mother duck would wait until Pippa almost reached her and then would fly off a few feet and lure my dog away from her brood.

This went on for several hours while I tried unsuccessfully to call my dog back to shore. I did not become concerned for my dog's safety until dusk started falling and the fishing boats began to appear. I knew the fishermen would never see Pippa in the half-light and could run into her and kill her. Our friends found someone on the lake with a boat that could take me out to where my dog was swimming. I will never forget the look on Pippa's face when I appeared right beside her. I told her sternly, "You go home," and she swam as quickly as she could to the shore. For the rest of the vacation, she still chased after the duck, but because she was convinced I walked on water, she came immediately whenever I called her.

Moral: Never forget that instinct overrides training.

One weekend we went to a state park known for some wonderful views across a river gorge. As well as the two Dachshunds and Harvey, we had also brought along a young Golden. It was a warm day, so we rolled the windows of the wagon down about five inches, to make sure the dogs had plenty of air. At one point, when we got out of the vehicle we decided it was safer to leave the dogs in the wagon because of a sheer drop of two hundred feet to the river below. This famous viewpoint had a four-foot-high stone wall around it to prevent anyone from falling over the edge into the ravine.

When we reached the wall, there were a number of visitors peering over the edge. Suddenly, to my horror, out of the corner of my eye I noticed our young Golden racing toward us. Somehow, he had managed to squeeze out of the window that we had left partially open. Before we had a chance to react, Wyant leapt up on top of the wall, where his momentum then carried him over the wall into the ravine below. Beneath the wall was nothing but scrubby bushes and rocks. There was a sound of crashing brush, then silence, and no sign of the dog. Dick tried to go over the wall after him, but the terrain was too steep, and there was no path. We stood there in a state of shock for several minutes, trying to decide on our next course of action. Were we going to try to recover the body, or had the dog fallen into the river and been swept away? Suddenly we heard heavy breathing and the noise of brush being disturbed, and Wyant reappeared about twenty feet below us, slowly working his way back up the ravine. While I hung onto Dick's legs he leaned over the wall and hauled the dog to safety. Wyant did not have a mark on him. The brush on the cliff must have broken his fall. We have no idea how far he fell before he managed to stop, but we had an experience that neither of us will ever forget.

Moral: Always remember that a dog can squeeze through a smaller space than you would expect.

One April morning, when the ice was just melting on the lakes, we took our four-month-old Golden for a walk in the forest preserve. The air temperature was just above freezing, and there was a brisk wind. Trucker suddenly spotted a flock of geese on the pond and started to chase after them. This did not concern us greatly at the time because a Golden Retriever should know how to swim, although Trucker had never been in the water before that day. Trucker got about fifty feet from shore and then started to sink. We called him, but he was panicking, his front legs flailing and his head almost under the water. Dick shouted to me, "Here, take my wallet and keys," as he kicked off his shoes and raced into the icy water. When he reached Trucker, he realized that the water was only three feet deep and the dog, during all this commotion, had his hind feet on the bottom of the pond. Dick grabbed him by the collar and dragged him to the shore. Our vehicle was parked some distance from the pond, and by the time we reached it, Dick's clothes were practically frozen to his body. We turned on the heater and raced for home. Dick told me later, in jest, that for a moment he almost considered drowning the dog when he realized Trucker could have walked out of the pond without his assistance.

Moral: Never take it for granted that your dog can swim.

C H A P T E R 2 2

Getting More out of Life, with Einstein

While the majority of dogs continue to fulfill their role of companion to man, others open up a whole new dimension of dog ownership for their human counterparts. In addition to being a companion, your dog can star in other roles. You and Einstein can become involved in a number of different activities. Some activities are open to all breeds, while others are limited to dogs of a specific genetic background. Perhaps Einstein has bonded with one of your children. Both children and adults can participate in many of the following activities, while, in addition, there are several 4-H projects in which dogs may participate with your children.

◄ Canine musical freestyle. If you ever dreamed of dancing with Fred Astaire, then perhaps you would enjoy dancing with Einstein. U-UD, Ch. OTCH Heelalong Jalapena UDX, HT, owned by Sandra Davis. *Photo by Bill Robinson. Border Collie, Herding Group.*

Dogs participating in performance events can do so even if they are neutered. Only beauty contests, or conformation shows as they are known, require your dog to be able to reproduce. If you want to do more with Einstein, there are many activities that you can do with a dog that is not able to be bred.

The fastest growing dog sport at the turn of the century is that of dog agility, which is open to both purebreds and mixed-breeds. Unfortunately, the American Kennel Club limits its agility trials to purebred dogs, but other organizations welcome **all** breeds of canines. Dog agility is a fast-paced sport, and dogs and their owners who participate in agility do so with enthusiasm. When you compete in agility, you run against the clock. The handler uses verbal commands and hand signals to direct his dog to run along a specified course. The route consists of numerous jumps, tunnels, and ramps, and the dog has to weave through a series of poles as well. Surprisingly enough, more than 25 percent of the human teams appear to be old enough to have AARP cards. Agility is an excellent way for both you and your dog to keep fit. A dog that responds to basic obedience commands and that is physically sound can be trained to run a novice agility course.

Some obedience trials are also open to all dogs, although the AKC has the same purebred requirements that it does for agility. Obedience trials are judged in a similar manner to ice-skating. There is a performance standard, and the judge scores the dog/handler team on how accurately they perform a specified routine. There are three levels of obedience, starting at the novice level and ending with utility. Obedience and agility trials are held in many areas of the country every weekend of the year.

If you ever dreamed of dancing with Fred Astaire or Ginger Rogers then perhaps you would enjoy dancing with Einstein. Canine musical freestyle (dancing with your dog) is a new activity open to all breeds and mixes. Dance routines are choreographed to music—classical, pop, jazz, or anything the handler chooses. Handlers wear costumes to portray the theme of the dance, and their dogs usually have matching neckwear. Routines are judged on technical execution and artistic impression, similar to ice-skating.

Women seem to dominate this sport, but men have also demonstrated some unique routines.

Tracking, a sport in which you put your dog on leash and he follows a scent, is another area where you can team up with your dog and enjoy the great outdoors. Tracking is not as popular as obedience or agility trials, and depending on where you live, finding the space required to lay a track can sometimes be difficult.

Two other performance events welcome dogs of all breeds and mixes. Flyball is a team event in which teams of four dogs run against each other in a relay race. Each dog jumps over a series of four low hurdles to reach a box, which the dog hits with his feet to release a tennis ball. Once the dog catches the ball, he turns around and races back over the jumps to the start line. Then the next dog in line is released by his handler to race to get another tennis ball. The heat is over when all four dogs on the team have each crossed the finish line with a ball, without missing any of the jumps. The team with the fastest time wins the heat. Each team runs against all other teams entered at that level, until one comes out the overall winner. However, flyball is not available in all areas of the country.

Finally, there are frisbee competitions, usually sponsored by one of the major dog food manufacturers. Athletic dogs fly through the air with what appears to be the greatest of ease, to catch a frisbee thrown by their handlers. Judges score the dogs on the difficulty of their leaps until one is crowned champion.

As you know, over the centuries dogs have been genetically programmed to behave in a certain manner. Often this genetic programming lies dormant under the surface and is only brought to the forefront when your dog is stimulated by outside forces. There are many activities available for dogs of specific breeds.

Herding breeds can participate in sheepdog trials, or herding tests, depending on the dog's level of expertise. Many of these trials are sponsored by Border Collie organizations, while others are sponsored by the AKC or the Australian Shepherd Club of America. Surprisingly, two breeds that you do not associate with herding are permitted to participate in AKC herding trials and tests—Samoyeds and Rottweilers. Many of the herding breeds retain some herding instinct, but finding livestock on which to work your dog is difficult for many pet owners. Herding clubs are located in many parts of the country, and members of these clubs often have access to livestock.

Sporting breeds can take part in retriever trials, spaniel trials, or pointing dog trials. There are even private hunting clubs where you can take your dog. Lure coursing is offered for sight hounds, while some of the scent hounds can participate in rabbit hunting or coon dog trials. In addition to hunting rabbits, the Dachshund may join the smaller terriers in earth dog trials. Dogs participating in these "den" trials have to "go to ground" down a long and twisting tunnel, to locate a "caged" rat. The tunnel is made out of wood, and the rat is fully protected from the dogs. This is probably one of the few times your terrier would get to do the work for which he was bred, unless you live in a rural area and have a barn on your property.

If you live in the frozen North and own a sled dog, you may decide to abandon your snowmobile and become a "musher." Another activity you can do when the snow is waist-high is to take your dog snowshoeing. If you like to swim, there are water trials for Newfoundlands and Portugese Water Dogs. These trials require that you actually go swimming with your dog, a unique experience. Some of the larger and stronger breeds, like Malamutes, can take part in weight-pulling contests. These events are usually found at dog shows and in particular at National Specialties, where a large number of one particular breed congregates at one time.

If you own one of the dogs considered a protection breed, like a German Shepherd or Rottweiler, you can train your dog for Schutzhund. A Schutzhund dog is considered "the total dog" because he competes in three areas—tracking, obedience, and protection. Women compete in this sport, side by side with men.

Watching your canine companion suddenly take an interest in doing something he was bred to do centuries ago is an exciting feeling for any dog owner. Being able to give your dog that opportunity is payback for all the pleasure he brings to you.

Perhaps you are looking for something you and Einstein can do for mankind. Some well-trained dogs visit patients at hospitals and nursing homes. It has been scientifically proven that visiting pets of any kind aid in the recovery of sick or depressed people. Many residents of nursing homes and retirement communities miss the companionship of a pet and look forward to the weekly visit of a "therapy dog." There are never enough dogs to fill this role, so if you like to volunteer to help people, you might want to consider training Einstein toward this end. Many people would appreciate his services.

Another area where dog can help mankind is in the area of search and rescue. When disaster strikes, or someone is lost in the wilderness, when it comes to finding a person alive it is often a dog that makes the difference between success and failure. Because of his size, you can send a dog into places too small for man to enter. In view of the fact that a dog has such amazing olfactory powers, he is the ideal tool to use to locate people in a disaster area, like in the rubble of an earthquake. Police and sheriff's departments often call on search and rescue groups to aid them in the search for missing persons, particularly children who might have wandered off. Perhaps this would be something that you and Einstein could do to help your fellow man. Search and rescue groups are to be found in many towns all over the United States, and they are always looking for volunteers.

Rainbow Bridge

(AUTHOR UNKNOWN)

Just this side of heaven is a place called Rainbow Bridge. When an animal dies that has been especially close to someone here, that pet goes to Rainbow Bridge. There are meadows and hills for all of our special friends so they can run and play together. There is plenty of food and water and sunshine, and our friends are warm and comfortable.

All the animals who have been ill and old are restored to health and vigor; those who were hurt or maimed are made whole and strong again, just as we remember them in our dreams of days and times gone by. The animals are happy and content, except for one small thing; they each miss someone very special to them, who had to be left behind. They all run and play together, but the day comes when one suddenly stops and looks into the distance. His bright eyes are intent; his eager body begins to quiver. Suddenly he begins to run from the group, flying over the green grass, his legs carrying him faster and faster.

You have been spotted, and when you and your special friend meet, you cling together in joyous reunion, never to be parted again. The happy kisses rain upon your face, your hands again caress the beloved head, and you look once more into the trusting eyes of your pet, so long gone from your life but never absent from your heart.

Then together you and your special pet cross the Rainbow Bridge. . . .

Epilogue

If you take the time to read this book from cover to cover and then use the ideas presented within these pages, you and Einstein should not only survive puppyhood but should also form a close and lasting bond. As his human partner you should also gain a better understanding of all things canine and learn what it takes to become a responsible dog owner. With luck, you will enjoy the companionship of Einstein for many years to come.

If you have children, the gift you can teach them is to love and respect Man's Best Friend. Remember that your children are dog's future. Dog has walked alongside man since time immemorial and will continue on this journey as long as man needs a friend. All man needs to do to further the relationship is to take time to teach dog the right way to live.

◄ This story is told for all who have lost, or who will someday lose, a special pet. Although they are no longer with us, we hold them forever in our hearts. In memory of Sweep, our special dog, 8/24/85 to 6/1/99.

Index

Kay Guetzloff and her Heelalong Border Collies—"Lava": OTCH Lava UDX, MX, MXJ, PT, "Wyn": Wyn CDX, OA, OAJ, "Sweep": OTCH Sweep UDX, AX, AXJ, "Kite": CH/OTCH Kite UDX, MX, MXJ, PT. *Author photo by Shary Singer.*

For more than thirty years, **Kay Guetzloff's** life has gone to the dogs. Kay and her husband and fellow trainer, Dick, owned and trained Obedience Trial Champion Heelalong Chimney Sweep, Utility Dog Excellent, Agility Dog Excellent, and Agility Jumpers Excellent—the top-ranked obedience dog of the twentieth century. Kay also owns Heelalong Dog Obedience and Agility School in San Angelo, Texas.

Born and raised in England, Kay immigrated to the United States in 1965. A puppy soon joined the family, and a career in dogs developed shortly thereafter. Although Kay's main interest was in training dogs, she also became a dog groomer, breeder, and kennel owner. Through her dealings with dogs in training, grooming, and boarding situations, she has gained vast experience with the various breeds and the problems that can occur when the lifestyle of the owner doesn't fit the dog. The topics covered in this book are taken both from her personal experience and from experience gained from working with dogs belonging to her clients.

Although Kay's interest lies in teaching a pet dog "the right way to live," she and her Border Collies also compete successfully in obedience, agility, and herding competitions across the country. Kay is one of few trainers in the United States to have put obedience titles on dogs out of all seven AKC groups.